THE STEVE HOWE GUITAR COLLECTION

BY STEVE HOWE, WITH TONY BACON
PHOTOGRAPHY BY MIKI SLINGSBY

CONTENTS

The Steve Howe Guitar Collection
By Steve Howe, with Tony Bacon

Published in the U.S. by Miller Freeman Books,
600 Harrison St., San Francisco, CA 94107
ISBN 0-87930-290-9

Publ..ress Ltd,

ISBN 871547-64-4

A catalogue record for this book is available from the British Library.

Printed in Hong Kong

Art Direction & Design: Nigel Osborne
Editor: Roger Cooper

Typesetting by Midford Limited, London W1
Print and Origination by Regent Publishing Services

94 95 96 97 5 4 3 2 1

INTRODUCTION

In the 34 years I have been playing the guitar I've built up a working collection of guitars designed to be used and played and applied to my music. This book documents that collection.

Every guitar that I've bought has been important to me. The collection is very much alive, always fluctuating and adapting to my current tastes and needs. Among the collection, there are clearly guitars that stand out. My Gibson ES175D, the very first Gibson which I bought, back in 1964, is my ultimate guitar. And for a long while my 1953 Martin 000-18 was the most sensational acoustic guitar ever. But I'm constantly discovering fresh musical areas to investigate as instruments surface in the collection, providing new voices through which my music can speak.

At the back of the book I've listed various friends and acquaintances who've helped me on my musical quest. I'd also like to thank anyone I've forgotten, and the record-buying and concert-going public who have supported my endeavours.

One's success often inhibits others from giving their honest opinions. I am therefore indebted to my wife Janet for her support and encouragement through the years, and her ability to be critical and yet constructive regarding my recordings and compositions.

I hope that you enjoy this book, and that it communicates my enthusiasm and love for the guitar in all its fascinatingly varied forms.

STEVE HOWE, SEPTEMBER 1993, DEVON, ENGLAND.

● *THE IN CROWD* (left). Also in the group were Keith West, Junior Wood, Simon Alcot and Ken Lawrence.

Tomorrow A psychedelic update of The In Crowd with Twink (drums), Junior Wood (bass), Keith West (vocal) and me (guitar). Tracks: My White Bicycle; Colonel Brown; Claremont Lake; Real Life Permanent Dream; Shy Boy;

● *DELANEY & BONNIE* After I left Bodast I played in PP Arnold's backing band on Delaney & Bonnie's European tour, and that was a very important experience. I rubbed shoulders with a lot of big names: Eric Clapton was playing with Delaney & Bonnie, as was George Harrison for a while. Something about that tour shaped me, and in some ways it prepared me for Yes.

The In Crowd This was my second group, with vocalist Keith West, who I went on to work with in Tomorrow. I came in to replace guitarist Les Jones. The group had already had a Top 30 hit with 'That's How Strong My Love Is' in May 1965.

I actually appeared on two singles: 'Stop! Wait A Minute'/'You're On Your Own', which came out in September 1965, and 'Why Must They Criticise'/'I Don't Mind', which was released some two months later.

Teenage Opera I worked as a session guitarist with producer Mark Wirtz, who then produced Tomorrow. One of the biggest hits before that was 'Excerpt From A Teenage Opera (Grocer Jack)' by Keith West, on which I also played on the B-side 'Theme From A Teenage Opera'. This single reached number two in the UK charts in 1967. I also played guitar on two further Keith West singles, 'Sam'/Thimble Full Of Puzzles' (released November 1967) and 'On A Saturday'/ 'The Kid Was A Killer' (July 1968).

Revolution; The Incredible Journey Of Timothy Chase; Auntie Mary's Dress Shop; Strawberry Fields Forever; Three Jolly Little Dwarfs; Now Your Time Has Come; Hallucinations.

● *YES GIGS* I'd joined Yes in the spring of 1970, after a phone call from Chris Squire, and the new line-up quickly entered into an intensive period of rehearsals. On 17th July 1970 I played one of my first gigs with the group at the Lyceum, in central London, which was a big rock venue at that time.

● *GIBSON ES175D* (left). This was my very first Gibson guitar. It had to be ordered specially from Gibson in the States for me by the Selmer music shop in London in 1964.

1963	1964	1965	1966	1967	1968	1969
A M J J A S O N D	J F M A M J J A S O N D	J F M A M J J A S O N D	J F M A M J J A S O N D	J F M A M J J A S O N D	J F M A M J J A S O N D	J F M A M J J A S O N D	J F M A

Syndicats I started playing with The Syndicats in 1963, when I was 16. We began as an R&B outfit, later becoming more blues-based. Our three singles were produced by Joe Meek, and were released on the Columbia label. I'm on 'Maybellene'/'True To Me' (March 1964); 'Howlin' For My Baby'/'What To Do' (January 1965) and the A-side of 'On The Horizon'/'Crawdaddy Simone' (September 1965).

● An early snap of me playing my Gibson 175 on-stage with The In Crowd (above), probably taken some time during 1966.

● Bodast's LP, produced by Keith West in 1969, was unreleased until the 1980s. I remixed the tapes for this 1988 version (above).

Bodast This group was originally a power trio with Bobby Clarke (drums), Dave Curtiss (bass) and me on guitar. We took the name Bodast from the first two letters of each of our forenames – and we were also briefly called Canto. Vocalist Clive Skinner joined, and bassist Bruce Thomas was a later addition. I nearly joined The Nice to replace David O'List, but Bodast talked me out of it. We recorded an album (see left) but split up later in 1969.

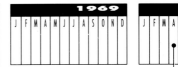

Yes guitar The original line-up of Yes had been together since the summer of 1968: Jon Anderson (vocal), Chris Squire (bass), Bill Bruford (drums), Tony Kaye (organ) and Pete Banks (guitar), and they recorded two albums. Banks' last appearance with Yes was at Luton on 18th April 1970, and I joined soon after.

● *EARLY DAYS* I was born in Holloway, north London, on 8th April 1947, and I received my first guitar, an acoustic with f-holes, as a present from my parents at Christmas 1959. In the early 1960s I moved on to electric guitars by Guyatone (right), Burns, and Gibson (above). My first recording was with The Syndicats, a single of 'Maybellene' (see label, above) and 'True To Me' which was released in March 1964. It was produced by Joe Meek, probably Britain's first independent record producer, and the maker of 'Telstar' by The Tornados among other hits. Meek operated a famous makeshift studio above a shop close to my home in Holloway.

● 'Maybellene' by The Syndicats was on this 1964 compilation LP (above).

● My first solid electric guitar was by Guyatone (below), a Japanese maker.

First tours Starting early in 1971 we toured Europe, supporting US band Iron Butterfly. It was very important for Yes, not least in terms of our live sound: after the tour we bought Butterfly's PA system, one of the earliest to use cinema-style 'bins' and 'horns'. Our tour manager Mickey Tait said that it made us sound "better than anyone in Europe". Later in 1971 we went on our first US tour, supporting Jethro Tull, Mountain and others.

● Yes 1971: Kaye; Squire; Anderson; Bruford; Howe.

The Yes Album My first studio experience with Yes took place at Advision studios in London toward the end of 1970, co-produced by the band and Eddie Offord. The result definitely took Yes on to a new musical level. Tracks: Yours Is

No Disgrace; Clap; Starship Trooper: Lifeseeker, Disillusion, Würm; I've Seen All Good People: Your Move, All Good People; A Venture; Perpetual Change.

Two more albums In the middle of 1972 I was at Advision again with co-producer Eddie Offord for my third album with Yes, Close To The Edge. Tracks: Close To The Edge: The Solid Time Of Change, Total Mass Retain, I Get Up I Get Down, Seasons Of Man; And You And I: Cord Of Life, Eclipse, The Preacher The Teacher, Apocalypse; Siberian Khatru. We moved to Morgan studios in north London in the later half of 1973 for Topographic, which became a double album. Tracks: The Revealing Science Of God: Dance Of The Dawn; The Remembering: High The Memory; The Ancient: Giants Under The Sun; Ritual: Nous Sommes Du Soleil.

● Playing and singing on-stage (above) on one of the dates of the Topographic Oceans tour in late 1973.

Yes keys Rick Wakeman had not been too happy with the Tales From The Topographic Oceans project, and he left Yes in May 1974. We did try Vangelis as a potential replacement, but that really didn't work out. Then we met Patrick Moraz from a band called Refugee. Patrick worked out very well, and joined Yes in August 1974.

Beginnings My first solo album, recorded at Morgan and Advision studios, and on location at my home in north-west London on mobile recording gear. During the five years or so that I'd been in Yes there was very little time for anything else musically, and this album really was my solo beginning. It allowed me to expand, and I especially enjoyed working with an orchestra (arranged by Patrick Moraz). On one track I used members of the group Gryphon, to give a medieval flavour. Tracks: Doors Of Sleep; Australia; The Nature Of The Sea; Lost Symphony; Beginnings; Will O' The Wisp; Ram; Pleasure Stole The Night; Break Away From It All.

Going For The One Some preliminary work was done with Patrick Moraz before he left the band, but Rick Wakeman plays all the keyboard parts on the album. It was the first album we'd made without Eddie Offord, and it took about seven months to complete, in Montreux, Switzerland, which was by far the longest that Yes had taken to make an album. This was partly due to the fact that we'd all just recently made solo records, and perhaps had become a little too individually over-confident. But the resulting album was very good, I think, and is in fact one of my favourite Yes albums. Tracks: Going For The One; Turn Of The Century; Parallels; Wonderous Stories; Awaken.

1970	1971	1972	1973	1974	1975	1976	1977

Fragile We were back at Advision in London with co-producer Eddie Offord in summer 1971, recording another album. Tracks: Roundabout; Cans And Brahms; We Have Heaven; South Side Of The Sky; Five Per Cent For Nothing; Long Distance Runaround; The Fish (Shindleria Praematurus); Mood For A Day; Heart Of The Sunrise.

Yes keys Part of the reason organist Tony Kaye left just before we recorded Fragile was that we felt that we needed a wider keyboard picture. Rick Wakeman replaced Tony and provided that, bringing synths and Mellotrons into Yes.

Yes drums Bill Bruford left the band in July 1972 after four memorable years with Yes, in order to join Robert Fripp's King Crimson. We had no hesitation in recruiting Alan White as his replacement. Alan's an excellent drummer, and was already a friend of the band. He joined in August, going straight to work on the Close To The Edge tour.

America Our record company, Atlantic, asked Yes to record a special track for a compilation of their rock artists, The New Age Of Atlantic. We chose to make a cover version of Paul Simon's 'America' – very successfully, I felt. The track was one of Bill Bruford's last recordings with the band.

Yessongs Live tracks: Intro; Siberian Khatru; Heart Of The Sunrise; Perpetual Change; And You And I; Mood For A Day; Six Wives Of Henry VIII; Roundabout; I've Seen All Good People; Long Distance Runaround; The Fish; Close To The Edge; Yours Is No Disgrace; Starship Trooper.

● On-stage in Seattle (right), July 1975, during our seventh US tour, with my trusty Fender twin-neck steel before me.

● *SESSIONS* I worked on the Lou Reed LP (1972), Rick Wakeman's Six Wives of Henry VIII (1973) and Alan White's Ramshackled (1976).

Relayer We recorded this album at Chris Squire's house in Virginia Water, Surrey. Co-producer Eddie Offord moved in his mobile recording gear alongside the band, and we worked during the summer and early autumn of 1974. Tracks: The Gates Of Delirium; Sound Chaser; To Be Over.

Yesterdays Each member of the band made a solo album during 1975: there was my Beginnings (see above), Jon Anderson's Olias Of Sunhillow, Chris Squire's Fish Out Of Water, Patrick Moraz's i, and Alan White's Ramshackled. Atlantic must have decided they needed a Yes album to fill this gap, so they put together the first Yes compilation album, Yesterdays. It seems that the idea was to attract people who hadn't got the early Yes LPs. It featured 'America' (an edited version of the New Age Of Atlantic track), plus six tracks from the two albums Yes made before I joined (Looking Around/ Time And A Word/ Sweet Dreams/Then/ Survival/ Astral Traveller) and an early B-side called 'Dear Father'.

Yes keys We started work on the Going For The One album with Patrick Moraz, but he left at the end of ·1976. I don't think Patrick was happiest in a group setting; he seemed more at home with solo projects. I was very excited when we then got Rick Wakeman back into the band, because I felt he was a more colourful and therefore more suitable keyboardist for Yes.

Tormato Not one of my favourites, although looking back now, 'Release Release', 'Silent Wings' and 'Madrigal' stand out from the rest. Backing tracks for Tormato were made at Advision, and we then moved over to Rak for overdubs and mixing. By the time Going For The One had come out, we'd stopped using Roger Dean for cover artwork – this was apparently done to give us a new visual direction. My feeling was that if it's working, don't turn it off. But a design company called Hipgnosis did the Going For The One and Tormato sleeves, and I must say that I dislike both. My original idea had been to call this album Tor – I'd found a map of Dartmoor with Yes Tor on it, and thought it would be a good idea to have a black-and-white shot of that on the cover. But for some reason Hipgnosis seemed to think that a squashed tomato was a much better idea. Tracks: Future Times; Rejoice; Don't Kill The Whale; Madrigal; Release, Release; Arriving UFO; Circus Of Heaven; Onward; On The Silent Wings Of Freedom.

Yes change We started recording for the next album late in 1979 in Paris with Roy Thomas Baker producing, but stopped after two months when Alan White broke a foot. Christmas intervened, after which we booked Redan studio in west London for three weeks, and only Chris Squire, Alan White and I turned up. It was beginning to become clear that Rick Wakeman and Jon Anderson were going to leave the band. Meanwhile, Chris told me how much he liked the Buggles record; I liked it too, and by March 1980 singer Trevor Horn and keyboardist Geoff Downes had joined Yes. We recorded Drama (right), the US tour was a great success, but European audiences were openly critical, especially about Jon's absence. In January 1981 the band finally split up.

Drama Sessions began with Eddie Offord co-producing at the Townhouse Studio in London, but after three weeks it was obvious that it wouldn't work with Eddie. Trevor Horn began helping on production, and we moved across London to Sarm East Studio, where Gary Langan and Julian Mendelsohn engineered the sessions – they were great to work with. I also enjoyed Geoff Downes' more settled keyboard approach, and it was fun working with some of his hi-tech gear, like the sampling Fairlight system. Tracks: Machine Messiah; White Car; Does It Really Happen?; Into The Lens; Run Through The Light; Tempus Fugit.

Asia Through my manager I met bassist John Wetton. We began to write and recruited Carl Palmer on drums. We thought about adding a singer, but I suggested Geoff Downes – and Asia was born.

Asia & Alpha The first song John Wetton and I wrote together was 'Without You', then 'One Step Closer' (which was mainly my song with John rewriting some of the lyrics) and 'Here Comes The Feeling' (this time it was John's song with some sections of mine added). Later, the Downes/Wetton team wrote songs like 'Heat Of The Moment'. We went on to record Asia at Marcus and Townhouse Studios, London, and the producer on the sessions was Mike Stone. Tracks: Heat Of The Moment; Only Time Will Tell; Sole Survivor; One Step Closer; Time Again; Wildest Dreams; Without You; Cutting It Fine; Here Comes The Feeling. We made Alpha at Le Studio in Montreal, Canada, with producer Mike Stone again, and engineer Paul Northfield. Tracks: Don't Cry; The Smile Has Left Your Eyes; Never In A Million Years; My Own Time (I'll Do What I Want); The Heat Goes On; Eye To Eye; The Last To Know; True Colours; Midnight Sun; Open Your Eyes.

Asia bass John Wetton left Asia after Alpha; we replaced him with Greg Lake. We played with Greg on a live MTV special, but he didn't last long, and John came back. He then called a meeting and said he couldn't work with me.

I smiled, said goodbye, and shortly after formed GTR. The record company later asked me to play on the Astra album, and although I was willing once I actually heard the tracks I decided not to participate in the project.

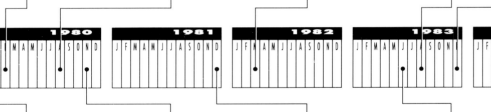

1978	1979	1980	1981	1982	1983	1984	1985
A M J J A S O N D	J F M A M J J A S O N D	J F M A M J J A S O N D	J F M A M J J A S O N D	J F M A M J J A S O N D	J F M A M J J A S O N D	J F M A M J J A S O N D	J F M A M J J A S O N

Montreux In the summer of 1979 I played a solo concert at the Montreux Jazz Festival in Switzerland, which was a rare and welcome opportunity for me to air some of the pieces from my solo albums. I also included material like 'Clap' and 'Mood For A Day' that I played regularly in my solo spots on Yes dates. I've always liked bluesman Big Bill Broonzy's playing, so I put in a cover of his 'The Glory Of Love' too. I was happy with my performance, and a video of it has recently been released in Japan.

Steve Howe Album My second solo record gave me even more opportunities to expand musically, outside of Yes. I did further work with an orchestra, this time using arrangements by Andrew Pryce Jackman. Among the other musicians I used on the album were Bill Bruford (drums), Clive Bunker (percussion), Claire Hamill (vocal), Ronnie Leahy (keys) and Alan White (drums). I produced the album in London at Rak studio, Redan studio, and EMI Abbey Road. Tracks: Pennants; Cactus Boogie; All's A Chord; Diary Of A Man Who Disappeared; Look Over Your Shoulder; Meadow Rag; The Continental; Surface Tension; Double Rondo; Vivaldi's Concerto In D (Second Movement).

Yesshows At the end of 1980, after Drama had come out, Atlantic Records decided to release Yes's second live album, Yesshows – which in fact had first been scheduled to come out a year earlier. The live tapes used for the record, originally released as a two-LP set, featured two line-ups with vocalist Jon Anderson. Some tracks had Rick Wakeman on keyboards and – from even earlier live tapes – some had Patrick Moraz ('The Gates Of Delirium', for example, features Moraz). Tracks: Parallels; Time And A Word; Going For The One; The Gates Of Delirium; Don't Kill The Whale; Ritual; Wonderous Stories.

Classic Yes Not long after the dissolution of the Trevor Horn/Geoff Downes line-up of Yes at the start of 1981, Atlantic must have decided that they needed to have some kind of 'new' Yes release. So the record company had Chris Squire put together this second compilation album of Yes material. Tracks: Heart Of The Sunrise; Wonderous Stories; Yours Is No Disgrace; Starship Trooper; Long Distance Runaround; The Fish (again!); And You And I; Roundabout; I've Seen All Good People.

● SESSIONS Although I was very busy with my own bands and projects in the early 1980s, I still found time to do a few selected sessions. I guested on

Cinema Alan White and Chris Squire pressed on together after Yes split in early 1981, and began to formulate a new group which they called Cinema, recruiting former Yes organist Tony Kaye, and a South African guitarist, Trevor Rabin. Jon Anderson also joined this line-up and they called themselves Yes, and lasted from 1983 to 1988.

The Dixie Dregs' album Industry Standard (1982) after meeting and jamming with their guitarist Steve Morse. When I'd first heard him in

GTR I met Steve Hackett through my manager, once again. An important part of a manager's job is to make connections and keep them together. Steve and I had a fantastic time writing songs together for three months, after which we had the whole album. Then we met a lot of different musicians in order to put the band together, and selected the most suitable players for GTR. The line-up we chose was: Max Bacon (vocal), Phil Spalding (bass) and Jonathan Mover (drums). Later, keyboardist Matt Clifford joined us on stage. We rehearsed the material for the album, Arista signed us, and we went into Townhouse-4 to make the album (for more details see right).

the late 1970s I really felt I was hearing a new generation of guitarist coming through again, and I still admire his playing and recordings.

● Live with Anderson Bruford Wakeman Howe (right) in 1989. We were usually augmented on-stage by Tony Levin (bass), Milton McDonald (guitar) and Julian Colbeck (keyboards).

ABWH The Anderson, Bruford, Wakeman, Howe album was recorded at Air studios in Montserrat and London. Tracks: Themes: Sound, Second Attention, Soul Warrior; Fist Of Fire; Brother Of Mine; Birthright; The Meeting; Quartet: I Wanna Learn, She Gives Me Love, Who Was The First, I'm Alive; Teakbois; Order Of The Universe; Let's Pretend.

Symphonic Music Of Yes I'd planned an orchestral Yes record for years with keyboardist/arranger David Palmer; we finally made it for release in October 1993. Bill Bruford and I were the ex-Yes members involved, plus Jon Anderson. Tracks: Roundabout; Close To The Edge; Wonderous Stories; All Good People; Mood For A Day; Owner Of A Lonely Heart; Survival; Heart Of The Sunrise; Soon; Starship Trooper.

The Grand Scheme Of Things August 1993. Tracks: Grand Scheme; Desire; Blinded By Science; Beautiful Ideas; Valley Of Rocks; New World: Wayward Course; Reaching The Point; Common Ground; Luck Of The Draw; Civilisation; Passing Phase; Georgia's Theme; Too Much Is Taken; Maiden Voyage; Road To One's Self.

ABWH/Yes merger *There had been a dreadfully complex and very expensive business going on at this time about who owned the name 'Yes'. Bill Bruford and I would have been happy to continue as ABWH, but gradually it became clear that the consensus among the interested parties was to merge ABWH and the existing Yes. So ABWH didn't so much split up as become the Union line-up of Yes, which limped on until 1992.*

GTR split *After the album and tours, GTR returned to England... and we never saw Steve again. He seemed to have lost interest in the idea. We started a second album, with Robert Berry replacing Steve, and Nigel Glockler on drums, but it was never finished, and GTR broke up at the end of 1987.*

Projects (below) Guitar Speak (left) was an album organised by Miles Copeland to present the work of 12 different guitarists. I contributed a remake of a track called 'Sharp On Attack', which I had first recorded for GTR's aborted second LP. I also worked with Ultravox's keyboardist Billy Currie's on his solo Transportation (centre), and with Paul Sutin on his Seraphim album.

Yes Years A compilation over four CDs, this was soon reorganised as a 2-CD package, YesStory, covering the whole of Yes's career.

1986	1987	1988	1989	1990	1991	1992	199
F M A M J J A S O N D	J F M A M J J A S O N D	J F M A M J J A S O N D	J F M A M J J A S O N D	J F M A M J J A S O N D	J F M A M J J A S O N D	J F M A M J J A S O N D	J F M A M J J A S

GTR album Produced by Geoff Downes, whose synth know-how helped the guitar-synth theme. We intended it to be a guitar duet tour-de-force, but probably we were too gentlemanly for that. Tracks: When The Heart Rules The Mind; The Hunter; Here I Wait; Sketches In The Sun; Jekyll & Hyde; You Can Still Get Through; Reach Out (Never Say No); Toe The Line; Hackett To Bits; Imagining.

● An unused logo (below) made from guitars in my collection, devised with photographer Miki Slingsby.

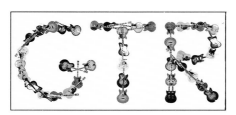

I also worked with Trevor Horn on Frankie Goes To Hollywood's Pleasure Dome (1984) and Liverpool (1986), and Propaganda's Secret Wish (1985).

ABWH formed *The idea for this group (Anderson, Bruford, Wakeman, Howe) first came to me via the business channels. Jon Anderson, who I hadn't worked with since he left the Yes line-up of 1979, wanted to get together again. He came to see me, and went away with a tape of my songs, including 'Brother Of Mine' and 'Birthright', and Jon started preliminary work in France. Later, I did my overdubs for the album at Air studio in London.*

● *SESSIONS During this period I worked with George Martin on Andy Leek's Say Something (1988), and played on Stanley Clarke's Animal Logic project (1989),* Queen's Innuendo (1991), and The Bee Gees' Size Isn't Everything (1993). I produced Martin Taylor's album Artistry (1992) at Langley, my Devon studio.

Speak live After the Guitar Speak album (above) a tour was organised under the Night Of The Guitar banner. A Live! album featured me solo on 'Clap', with Pete Haycock on 'Würm', and with the assembled cast on 'All Along the Watchtower'.

Union Tracks: I Would Have Waited Forever; Shock To The System; Masquerade; Lift Me Up; Without Hope; Saving My Heart; Miracle Of Life; Silent Talking; The More We Live; Dangerous; Holding On; Evensong; Take The Water To The Mountain.

● Union Yes (left): Rabin, Kaye, Wakeman, White, Squire, Anderson, Bruford, Howe.

Union *We began the recording of this album with good intentions, but the group mostly hated the result. Some say my 'Masquerade' was the best track: it cost only about £5 at my studio. The rest of the album cost some $2 million to make.*

Turbulence My third solo album; there's also a video, Turbulent Plan. Tracks: Turbulence; Hint Hint; Running The Human Race; Inner Battle; Novalis; Fine Line; Sensitive Chaos; Corkscrew; While Rome's Burning; From A Place Where Time Runs Slow.

Asia's Aqua I guested on: Aqua Pt 1; Who Will Stop The Rain?; Back In Town; Someday; The Voice Of Reason; Lay Down Your Arms. I toured Japan/Europe/US in 1992 and Canada/US in 1993.

THE GIBSON COLLECTION

175 body (above) I put earlier 'speed' knobs on, which are easier to grip. When I changed the machine-heads I used one of the old buttons to replace the normal selector switch, and I've since filed it down to an oblong shape.

Although my first electric guitars were a Guyatone (see p66) and a Burns Jazz, the Gibson ES175D was my very first Gibson guitar, and the start of a long love affair with Gibson guitars. Since buying my 175 new in 1964 from a guitar shop in London I've had the opportunity to visit the Gibson factory in the US many times, and I've also been able to order special custom instruments, one of which you can see here (see also p21). Gibson started making guitars at the end of the 19th century when Orville Gibson set up an instrument making workshop in Kalamazoo, Michigan. It was the sound and the beautiful hand-carved tops of Orville's mandolins that first caught players' attention, but the company's guitars gradually began to gain in popularity as well. I have many Gibsons in my guitar collection, and as we'll see over the first half of this book a good number of the ideas that now seem commonplace in guitar making were established or popularised by Gibson.

Backstage (above) Ever since as a teenager I asked a guitarist how he bent strings, I've used 012s for both first and second strings on my 175.

◼ GIBSON ES175D July 1964

Serial: 183488
ES175 produced 1949-current

HERITAGE SWEET 16

Gibson closed their original Kalamazoo factory in 1984 and moved to Nashville. I began to hear rumours that some of the Gibson craftsmen had stayed in Kalamazoo, because they liked making guitars there. Then I heard that they'd started a company called Heritage, set up in the old Gibson factory – and my appetite was whetted. I arranged to visit them while I was on tour in the States with Yes for the *Union* tour in 1991. I'd decided, in my 175 state of mind, that I'd like to buy a Sweet 16. The Heritage people were just so helpful – and then gave me the guitar! To be given one as good as this, that you want and are prepared to pay for, is very rare, and an honour. I recorded a piece called 'Sweet', funnily enough, all on the Sweet 16. I couldn't think of a title for it other than 'Sweet', and then I heard that my Auntie Dorothy had died, and I mentally dedicated it to her. I might call it 'Sweet D', 'Sweet Dorothy' or just 'Sweet'. It's not released yet, but it's an important piece, a little jazzier than my usual writing.

175 neck (above) I find these fingerboard inlays very attractive, and I've

been drawn to other Gibsons bearing the same style, such as the ES345 (see p16).

◼ GIBSON ES175D STEVE HOWE CUSTOM c1978

Serial: 327081

On tape (above) Playing the 175 in the studio at Montreux in Switzerland, in 1977, recording one of the tracks for the Going For The One album. We'd

all made solo records prior to that LP, and there was a slight feeling that each of us was still in his own camp. It took seven months to record Going For The One.

Steve Howe Custom (above) It has the pickups and controls of my Switchmaster plus the size and feel of my 175. I added the fine-tuning tailpiece, and I'm back to the original knobs after a few changes. At first I was disappointed because the guitar didn't seem to have the edge that I think the original stolen version had (see box, right), but I've gradually got to like it a little more. And so it's been on tour as a spare when I've occasionally used it instead of my 175, but it hasn't appeared on record.

Original Custom (above) This is all I have of my first blonde stolen custom.

STEVE HOWE CUSTOM

I'd been carrying my 175 and my Switchmaster on a few Yes tours, so around 1978 it seemed logical to order from Gibson a custom-built crossover of the two. The original was stolen from the airport just after it was finished, so what you see pictured above is really number two. They did a good job, especially in copying the feel of my 175 neck. I specified a Super 400 headstock inlay because you rarely see that anywhere else – and on reflection I think it would have looked better with 175-style fingerboard inlays. I added two extra frets – but that meant we couldn't get the same space between the end of the neck and the neck pickup as I have on my 175. Three pickups did turn out to be rather an interference, and I've since lowered the middle pickup to get it out of the way. In fact I'm thinking of putting a MIDI pickup in the middle position so that I can also use this guitar for synthesiser sounds.

Style U (below) *A big body – this one is nearly 19 inches wide – produced a big sound, which enjoyed some popularity in turn-of-the-century mandolin orchestras to support the bottom end of the ensemble sound.*

Style U neck *The very earliest Gibson harp guitars had 12 sub-bass strings connected to the extended 'neck', but ten gradually became standard, as on this instrument. The sub-bass strings are used to add sustained bass accompaniment to your normal playing on the six-string neck.*

GIBSON STYLE U harp guitar c1924

Serial: 79513
Style U harp guitar produced 1902-c1929

GIBSON'S ANTIQUES CORNER

The harp guitar is just an absolutely wonderful instrument, a gorgeous thing. At one time I would keep it at my house and I used to bash around on it regularly. It plays pretty well, but it's just such a terrific thing to collect – it cries out to be seen, and that really is a good part of the reason I bought it.

Ever since I knew they existed, I wanted one. Most of the inspiration came from seeing pictures of harp guitars in the *Gibson Story* book. I always hoped to get one like the reverse-scroll Orville Gibson harp guitar that's pictured in there, but I think there's only that one in existence – so the chances were remote!

Certainly the one I've got was the most expensive Gibson instrument in its day – in 1928, for example, it was listed at $300 retail, $25 more than the next most expensive Gibson, the L5. And it's a lovely example: very clean, very nicely refinished when I bought it, and it sounds absolutely enormous.

You play it just like an ordinary guitar, and I use the bass strings for sustain, you can't finger them. It's a bit of a monster. It's so big you have to lean over it and sort of play down on to it – you have to look down because it doesn't sit where you'd expect a normal guitar to be. To me it sounds big and honky, rather untamed. I have taken it along to studio sessions, all strung up and fully in tune, but it's never really made it on to any records. Not the most usable guitar, for sure, but I bought it very much as an interesting piece for the collection.

STYLE O AND MANDO-CELLO

I saw a picture of Big Bill Broonzy playing a Style O... and then I found out later that he didn't have one. People pose with this guitar. At first I couldn't believe it was a Gibson, because it doesn't look like your standard image of a Gibson. But I knew I had to have it as soon as I saw one in a dealer's shop.

At first I played the Style O quite a bit, because I was taking it on as a playing guitar. It has a quite nice rounded feel to the fingerboard and the neck has the typical V-shaped profile of the period. It sounds more like an f-hole archtop than a round-soundhole flat-top to my ears, and I must say that I rather like the look and feel of the 'flat' cutaway. I really appreciate this guitar, because it's an unusual Gibson in many ways.

The mando-cello has a lovely body shape, very well proportioned at this size. I've tried to get it in on a few recordings but it's never been quite 'there'. It might well be outside of what I need, and although I'm gradually getting my collection closer to practical needs, I'm always going to allow certain items purely on the strength of collectability.

One of the main sources of instruments in the collection at one time was a dealer in Nashville, Tennessee called George Gruhn, and all three instruments on these three pages came from him. I bought the harp guitar and the Style O for $750 apiece while on tour in the States with Yes, in the first half of 1974. The mando-cello was a slightly later purchase, at $800.

Harp guitar (right) A page from The Gibson Story, which was a basic history published by the company in 1973, and the place where I first learned of their harp guitars. This one was made by Orville Gibson around 1900, with some wonderful decorative work on the fingerboard and headstock.

EARLY GIBSONS

As the acoustic guitar became more important and commercially viable during the first quarter of the 20th century, the Gibson company began to apply the finer attributes of their successful mandolins to the larger six-string instrument, producing some classic guitars as a result. On these three pages you can see the part of the collection that I call my Gibson antiques, a group of fabulously striking instruments that were made at Gibson's Kalamazoo, Michigan workshops in the 1910s and 1920s.

Group (left) This is a useful shot to pore over the various differences and similarities. Two have a pearl dot in the scroll; one is without. Two have decorated soundhole rings; one is plain. And of course I've added usable machine heads to the Style O, the one I want to play.

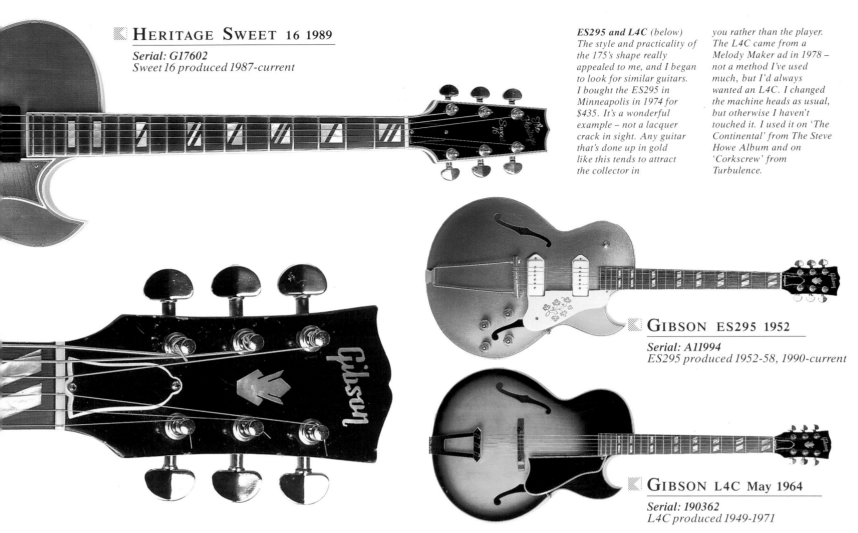

▨ HERITAGE SWEET 16 1989
Serial: G17602
Sweet 16 produced 1987-current

ES295 and L4C (below)
The style and practicality of the 175's shape really appealed to me, and I began to look for similar guitars. I bought the ES295 in Minneapolis in 1974 for $435. It's a wonderful example – not a lacquer crack in sight. Any guitar that's done up in gold like this tends to attract the collector in

you rather than the player. The L4C came from a Melody Maker ad in 1978 – not a method I've used much, but I'd always wanted an L4C. I changed the machine heads as usual, but otherwise I haven't touched it. I used it on 'The Continental' from The Steve Howe Album and on 'Corkscrew' from Turbulence.

▨ GIBSON ES295 1952
Serial: A11994
ES295 produced 1952-58, 1990-current

▨ GIBSON L4C May 1964
Serial: 190362
L4C produced 1949-1971

Custom (right) When Jon Anderson and Rick Wakeman left Yes early in 1980, we were joined by Trevor Horn and Geoff Downes; they'd had success before as Buggles. Here we are on stage in 1980: I'm playing my Steve Howe Custom ES175D.

THE PRIZED 175

The Gibson ES175D was my first Gibson, my first 'proper' guitar. I bought it new from Selmer's shop in London's Charing Cross Road in 1964; they had to order it specially from Gibson in the US. It cost 200 guineas (£210) and my dad helped me buy it on hire purchase.

I'd left school a few years earlier, and at the time I was in a blues group called The Syndicats – we recorded a few singles, produced by Joe Meek. I used to catch a number 14 bus from where I lived in Holloway, north London, and spend the day in the music shops in and around Charing Cross Road. I got to play many different guitars and met a lot of people that way. That was how I got the job with my next group, The In Crowd, in 1965, with vocalist Keith West. We turned into Tomorrow a few years later. I used my 175 right through this period, swapping occasionally with my Guyatone (see p66) when I wanted a different sound. But generally the 175 suited whatever turn of mood I had.

The desire for the 175 had taken years to accumulate, through

Gibson catalogues and magazines, and even believing that Wes Montgomery had played one because there's one on the cover of his album *The Incredible Jazz Guitar*. I really liked the look and the shape of the 175, the whole visual aspect, and thought it would be right for me. The fact that it was so scarce in Britain at the time and so few people seemed interested in the 175 almost helped me to want it. I often find that if other people haven't got something, then I might become interested in it.

I found the 175 so intriguing to look at, and when it first arrived I used to look at it a great deal. I stared at it, almost meditated with it. I would fantasise that this guitar would take me to a place where I wanted to go – as indeed it did. And I was fastidious about it: I cleaned it a lot, periodically I'd take everything off, the strings, the bridge, scratchplate and all, and clean the whole guitar. It would look astounding.

After Tomorrow split I did some sessions for a while, then in 1968 joined a shortlived group called Bodast, still using my 175. I remember in July 1969 we played the Albert Hall, supporting The Who and Chuck Berry. I got a chance backstage to ask Chuck what he thought of my 175. He picked it up, strummed it a bit, and said, "This is great, a lovely guitar." So I put the guitar back in the case and I felt really good: Chuck Berry's played my guitar! Not that he's a technical marvel, but he was the influence that made rock guitar really come alive.

YES AND THE 175

Early in 1970 I got a call from Chris Squire, and around April I joined Yes. There was no reason why I wasn't going to carry on playing my

175. The band accepted that it wasn't the normal kind of guitar people used in rock groups, but it was obvious that I loved it and was going to play it. We recorded *The Yes Album* at Advision studios, and that record pushed us to a much more demanding level. It was the first time I was in a group where we really used overdubbing properly. I play 175 on everything on *The Yes Album*, except the solos on 'Perpetual Change' where I use my Guyatone.

When I went to America for the first time with Yes in 1971 I was still in awe of my 175, and I carried it as if I was carrying the crown jewels. I'm exactly the same with it now. Nobody else touches the guitar, nobody else tunes it, nobody strings it: I've made it exclusively mine. The great danger of that is that some people around you can really worry about how obsessed you are. On that first tour of America I was only 24, it was a very big upheaval for me, and I felt totally estranged, almost in another universe – and I did actually sleep with the 175. There was no sexual contact! But I did sleep with the guitar.

The 175 has been very important to me ever since, and I've used it on many tracks, such as: 'Siberian Khatru' final solo *(Close To The Edge)*; 'Heart Of The Sunrise' *(Fragile)*; 'Lost Symphony' *(Beginnings)*; 'On The Silent Wings Of Freedom' *(Tormato)*; 'Hint Hint', 'The Inner Battle *(Turbulence)*; 'Big Dream' *(ABWH)*; 'Holding On' *(Union)*; 'The Fall Of Civilization' *(The Grand Scheme Of Things)*, and many, many more. I seem to go to other guitars to be someone else, like putting on a mask, and as we'll see in this book some guitars have come and gone in importance. But the Gibson ES175 is the guitar that I come back to when I want to find my true nature again.

GIBSON STYLE O c1918

Serial: 50634
Style O produced 1902-1923

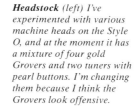

Headstock (left) I've experimented with various machine heads on the Style O, and at the moment it has a mixture of four gold Grovers and two tuners with pearl buttons. I'm changing them because I think the Grovers look offensive.

Style O (left) The arched top, oval soundhole and scroll decoration are typical of Gibson at that time. I've altered the bridge to improve the guitar's playability.

GIBSON K4 MANDO-CELLO c1919

Serial: unreadable
K4 mando-cello produced 1912-c1927

K4 mando-cello (above) If the mandolin was a violin and the mandola (see p14) a viola, then the low-pitched 14inch-wide K4 would have been a cello: hence Gibson's invented name, 'mando-cello'. Toward the end of the K4's life in the 1920s this parallel with the instruments of the orchestra was underlined in a Gibson catalogue, which enthused over the "charming new colorful effects secured with the quartet of mando-cello, mandola, and first and second mandolins".

F4 (left) This mandolin has Gibson's early 'three-point' body. The shape is seen on oval- or round-soundhole mandolins dated before about 1910, after which they adopt the 'two-point' shape (similar to the F5, right). The beautiful headstock decoration is made from abalone and wire inlays.

F5 (left) Introduced during the time that the renowned acoustic engineer Lloyd Loar worked for Gibson (1919-1924), the F5 is regarded as the epitome of mandolin design. It was originally part of the Master Model series launched in 1922, which also included the ground-breaking L5.

◁ GIBSON F4 mandolin c1908
F4 produced 1902-1943

◁ GIBSON F5 mandolin 1955
Serial: A21252 Factory order: W2074 I
F5 produced 1922-1980

MANDOLIN INTERLUDE

From about 1910 to the mid 1920s Gibson were best known for their excellent mandolins – guitars hardly got a look in. The best of their mandolins have an authentic bluegrass sound about them, and I've acquired several versions and types over the years as my interest in mandolins developed. There were three main influences that steered to me into playing more mandolin. I heard Vivaldi's wonderful mandolin concertos, and they sparked my initial interest. Then in the early 1970s the American group Seals & Crofts supported Yes at QPR football ground in England, and I admired their brilliant interplay of acoustic guitar, voices and Dash Crofts' mandolin. They were sometimes too middle-of-the-road for my taste, but they were clever at creating a texture, and the use of mandolin within that really pricked my ears. More recently, I've admired the work of David Grisman. He's been playing a very successful fusion of bluegrass and jazz in various live and recording projects, often teamed with one-time Grateful Dead guitarist Jerry Garcia.

Five Gibsons (above) From left to right: H1 mandola; F4 mandolin; F5 mandolin; Florentine electric mandolin; and A mandolin. The relative sizes can be appreciated from this group shot: note

especially the larger body of the mandola, designed to transmit the deeper tones of its lower-tuned strings. It's also interesting that the same headstock design is seen spanning 50 years on the three central mandolins.

▦ GIBSON FLORENTINE electric mandolin c1960
Florentine produced 1954-1971

Florentine (above) As Gibson introduced new electric guitars, the technology was also applied to their mandolin models. The ES150 f-hole electric guitar just preceded the EM150 electric mandolin (both 1936), while the Les Paul solid electric guitar (1952) was followed by the Florentine solid electric mandolin (1954).

Mandola (right) On the headstock is the Kalamazoo company's classic 'The Gibson' logo in elegant script lettering, which you can see repeated on the metal tailpiece down at the bottom of the body. Some early Gibson instruments omit a logo, like the F4 mandolin opposite.

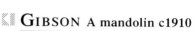

GIBSON A mandolin c1910

Serial: 13466
A produced 1902-1933

GIBSON H1 mandola c1918

Serial: 53541
H1 produced 1902-1936

Catalogue (above) The title page of an early 1920s Gibson brochure features film actress Priscilla Dean strumming one of Gibson's mandolins. Notice how in those days Gibson put Mandolin before Guitar in the official company name.

'A' mandolin (right) Two general body styles have been used by Gibson for their mandolins: the 'rounded' symmetrical shape, as seen on this model A, and the 'pointed' asymmetrical shape, used for example on the F5 and F4 models opposite. For stage work I've added a pickup linked to a socket taped to the pickguard bracket of the 'A'.

Mandola (left) Gibson called the mandola "the counterpart of the tenor banjo and the viola" and suggested a tuning a fifth below the mandolin. Gibson's larger mando-cello (see p13) was pitched an octave below mandola, while their huge, rare mando-bass was tuned like a modern bass guitar.

ACOUSTIC VS ELECTRIC

I used to play my F5 in the studio – it's on 'Birthright' on *ABWH* and some tracks on *Turbulence* – but I find it a little bass-light and harsh these days. Now I feel the F4 has more depth, and it's my key mandolin now. I recorded it first on the *Grand Scheme* album.

The mandola is interesting, but it's more of an experimental instrument. I first recorded the solid electric Florentine on *Beginnings,* notably the introduction to 'Lost Symphony'. It also turns up on the last section of 'Circus From Heaven' (*Tormato*), playing arpeggios and sounding something like a capo'd 12-string. I often used it on stage with Yes just for that part.

The plainer A-model was given to me by a very kind fan in Philadelphia in the 1970s. I didn't want to use my lovely studio mandolins on the road, so it provided me with the perfect live instrument – plus it has a wider fingerboard which means more manoeuvrability. I first played it on stage on the ABWH tour, and it made me feel I'd never play electric mandolin again.

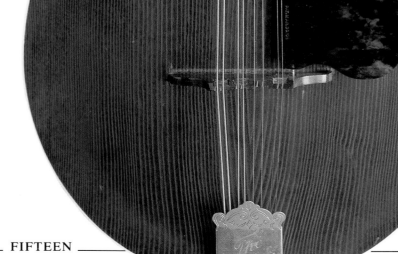

345 neck (below) The 345's fingerboard feels narrow and small, which I find gives me a terrific mobility. This guitar's always seemed as if it's built for adventure, and that makes it tremendously good for improvisational playing.

345 body (above) I played my 345 a lot in the 1970s. It got very worn, so Gibson overhauled it for me in 1982. They put a Byrdland-style tailpiece on with 'ES-345' inscribed on it, and it makes it look rather different, which I like.

Cover (right) This 1975 Beat Instrumental uses a live shot taken during the Topographic Oceans tour. Notice that at the time I had five 'speed' knobs on the 345, including one in place of the big black tone selector knob.

Round stage (left) Yes played in the round on the Tormato and Drama tours, from 1978 to 1980. As well as the 345 that I'm playing, I have my Portuguese 12-string, Martin 00-18, Kohno, Fender twin-neck steel, The Les Paul, Rickenbacker 12-string, Telecaster and Florentine mandolin.

345 live (right) Here's the 345 in action on the Close To The Edge tour at the Crystal Palace Bowl in London, probably in 1973.

GIBSON ES345TD 1971

Serial: 632687
ES345TD produced 1959-1981

The 345 sound *(below) The 345 is wired for stereo output. If you hook it up to two amps, the back pickup comes out from one speaker and the warm pickup from the other. I* then put distortion on the left and a clean delay on the right, and the guitar comes alive. When you're in between those two speakers you hear one hell of a guitar sound – I hope it projects!

Gibson ad *(above) I did this for Gibson's UK agent Selmer in 1971. In return they gave me the lovely walnut Gibson ES345 stereo guitar (left).*

GIBSON ES335-12 January 1967

Serial: 860522
ES335-12 produced 1965-1971

335-12 *(below) I have this tuned a fifth below normal, giving me a deep-pitched 12-string. I don't use it too much, but I find it useful to know that I have such a different tone colour to hand if I should need it.*

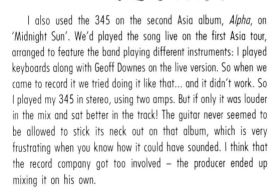

CLOSE TO THE EDGE WITH THE 345

The 345 was the first of the thinline-body Gibson electrics that I acquired. Gibson gave it to me in 1971 in return for an ad I did for them. It's one of the most exciting Gibsons I've ever played, and I used it as the predominant guitar on the recording of *Close To The Edge* in 1972.

The great thing about the guitar was the accessibility of the neck. We were playing hurtling riffs, very fast. On my trusty ES175 I wanted to play more like I did on *The Yes Album*, homespun ideas. Somehow, when I put this new guitar in my hands I felt like a new guitarist. It played beautifully, like a Les Paul Custom, with a very small neck. I sometimes think of this guitar as if it were an enormous landing sight for my fingers; everywhere you land you can go somewhere else. It's tremendous when you feel that potential, when you know you can leave all the garbage behind you. The stereo effect that the 345 has can sound terrific, and then there's a Vari-tone five-way select switch, like a tone selector but really only usable on two alternate positions. I use one of those for my rhythm sound, and the next for my lead sound. It also acts as a sort of volume boost.

I liked the way that I began to change my guitars as the image of Yes changed – the clothes, the sound and the concept of each album all changed as we went along – and for me that really started with the 345 and *Close To The Edge*. I've used the 345 since then, on stage of course, but also on side one of *Topographic*, and also on tracks such as 'Silent Talking' on *Union*.

I also used the 345 on the second Asia album, *Alpha*, on 'Midnight Sun'. We'd played the song live on the first Asia tour, arranged to feature the band playing different instruments: I played keyboards along with Geoff Downes on the live version. So when we came to record it we tried doing it like that... and it didn't work. So I played my 345 in stereo, using two amps. But if only it was louder in the mix and sat better in the track! The guitar never seemed to be allowed to stick its neck out on that album, which is very frustrating when you know how it could have sounded. I think that the record company got too involved – the producer ended up mixing it on his own.

THE MURKY 335-12

I have a friend called Paul Sauerteig, a lawyer, who occasionally turns up interesting guitars for me – and this was one of them. I now have it set up in an interesting way, and it's become one of a few instruments I have that I call 'project' guitars.

The 335-12 is set up a fifth below a guitar, so when you play open E on the bottom string, for example, you actually hear low B. The overall effect is very pleasing, with a very low, murky 12-string sound. It has some disadvantages: I had to put gaffer tape across the strings behind the bridge to stop them rattling, as it's strung so low, and I'm always fiddling with the string gauges. But plugged into a Marshall it sounds incredibly powerful. I haven't used it a great deal, but it does the stab chords in the chorus of 'Only Time Will Tell' on the first Asia album, plus various other tracks.

Blonde Artist (below) This was a specially ordered guitar that Gibson made for me, because the Artist wasn't normally available in this blonde finish. I think the natural wood really suits the guitar.

GIBSON ES ARTIST June 1980

Serial: 81630009
ES Artist produced 1979-1985

Sunburst Artist (below) The ES Artist transplanted the expanded-tone electronics of Gibson's unpopular RD guitars into the more familiar body style of the company's 335-style models.

Cover (right) An ES Artist live with Asia on a 1983 copy of this magazine.

THE GIBSON CREST

Here's an example of a guitar acquiring a reputation for rarity and luxuriousness, but not actually delivering as a playing instrument. I bought it in 1979 from a place called Silver Strings in St Louis, for $1000, and I can date its manufacture accurately because there's an inspection tag with it from March 1970. I had heard that Crests sounded rather good because of the Brazilian rosewood body, and it does sound rather nice – a bit like a Gibson Johnny Smith, I suppose, because it has those similar tiny pickups on it. But it

drives me nuts not being able to get anywhere on it. The way the neck joins the body at the 16th fret (like Gibson's ES330) is quite catastrophic, because you can't use the frets above F-sharp or so, and that just is not good enough for guitarists like me, or in fact any kind of guitarist who's used to having some kind of accessibility. Even on the 175, bless its heart, you can get to a high C easily. So I would say that the Crest is a badly designed juncture of neck and body – despite everything else about it being rather nice. It's just a bit too mellow for me.

THE ARTIST'S ELECTRONICS

The Artist used similar electronics to those that Gibson had used in their unusually-shaped RD guitars. They'd given me one of those to try out when we were starting to record *Tormato* in London in 1978, but I didn't like the styling.

The first ES Artist I got was the sunburst one. Pat Aldworth, the artist relations guy at Gibson, brought it to me on one of the gigs on Yes's US *Drama* tour in 1980 – the Yes-meets-Buggles episode, which was great fun. So I got up on stage after the soundcheck, plugged it in, and I was saying: Oh! What does this switch do? Pat told me that one switch was a limiter, and I'd always wanted one of those on a guitar. It stops you overloading the amplifier. Even so, I always had to use a volume pedal in combination with the Artists, otherwise they'd scream at me.

The double pickguards are something I had done specially. I felt that, because the Artist had no f-holes, it looked somehow unfinished and bare. So the extra pickguard seems to finish it off a

GIBSON ES ARTIST April 1982

Serial: 81162043
ES Artist produced 1979-1985

Gibson poster (right) I was voted top guitarist in America's Guitar Player magazine every year from 1978 to 1982. This celebratory 1981 poster features the sunburst ES Artist model.

GIBSON CREST GOLD March 1970

Serial: 850441
Crest produced 1969-1972

STEVE HOWE

OVER ALL BEST GUITARIST

GIBSON
ES ARTIST PLAYER

Guitar
PLAYER
POLL WINNER

Crest Gold (above) A luxurious guitar, having a multiple-bound body and scratchplate made from expensive Brazilian rosewood. The Gold version was set off by gold-plated hardware (there was also a Crest Silver version) and in 1970 it cost $900 new, twice the price then of an ES335.

ES Artists live (right) A shot from an Asia concert in the early 1980s, when I really got into using the ES Artists – here I'm using no less than four! You can see that I'm playing a tobacco sunburst model, and there are three behind me: the sunburst and blonde models, plus another finished in black.

little better to my eye. I'm sure I'd seen a guitarist in a picture years ago with a blonde 335 with twin pickguards, and I'd made a mental note at the time that it looked good.

Effectively what you had in the Artist was a more hi-fi guitar, with a limiter, expander, and treble boost. Another of its advantages was that you could make internal adjustments to control the sound, and I liked the fact that there's only one overall volume control. The Artist had a crystal clear top end, and to me the whole instrument shouts 'classic Gibson' – a super guitar. Very beautiful. It has every angle covered.

But very few players picked up on the ES Artist. I think Bob Weir in the Grateful Dead bought one. Bob seemed a bit like me, he'd always buy the latest idea. I remember hearing that he also acquired one of Gibson's special The Les Pauls (see p34).

ARTIST IN ASIA

The Artist became the guitar that I used in Asia, it seemed the right kind of instrument for that group. 'Cutting It Fine' on *Asia* is quite adventurous because I play the sunburst Artist all the way through in a live way. We'd already recorded the song and I had to put on the guitar, but instead of overdubbing, I went for the whole song, using a pedalboard which I don't usually do in the studio, with two amps and a live sound.

When it came to the Asia tour I decided that I wasn't going to take dozens of guitars around with me, I was tired of all that. So I ordered a few more Artists – and I ended up with four! I was completely obsessed with these guitars. I wanted something that was clean and simple, really streamlined, so that I didn't have to mess about. That's the kind of group Asia was – less messing about, just getting on with things.

John Wetton left Asia after *Alpha* (1983) and we decided to get in Greg Lake. We rehearsed for three weeks in Japan just to play an MTV live special. I had the four Artists, and they were all tuned to varying degrees of flatness because Greg didn't want to sing the

songs so high. I didn't want to change my guitar parts, because a lot of the quality of the voicing is often dependent on your positioning on the fingerboard. So I simply used some of the guitars at lower pitches. One was tuned to normal pitch, with another as backup, and then one was a semi-tone down and one a whole tone down. Greg also wanted the lyrics on autocue, because he said there were too many to remember, so on the *Asia In Asia* video you can see him looking down a lot!

Back off tour, I got to thinking about my guitars, and I figured that four Artists really was a hell of a lot of Artists! So I decided to sell the tobacco sunburst version. But the plans with Greg Lake came to nothing, because when we got home a rift had opened up in the band. Before we knew it, in spring 1984, we were back to getting John to return. We rehearsed for two weeks in London, which were harmonious. But then John called a meeting and said he couldn't work with me. I got up and smiled, and said goodbye. A few months later I formed GTR with Steve Hackett.

GIBSON STEVE HOWE CUSTOM Sept 1980

Serial: 001

Label *(right) Signed to me "from all your friends at Gibson": Pat Aldworth, Gary Aumaugher, Bruce Bolen, Charles Burge, Maudie Moore, Tim Shaw, Lori Stoltman, Rendal Wall and Abraham Wechter. Its dated 10th September 1980.*

Construction *(right) My snapshot shows the body of the Steve Howe Custom taking shape in the Gibson workshops at Kalamazoo during 1980. The clamps at the end of the body are to hold a glued section together until bonded.*

THE STEVE HOWE CUSTOM

Pat Aldworth at Gibson put me in touch with a guitar maker there called Abe Wechter. He helped me to design the model, and I'd told him that what I wanted was a deluxe Country Western model. The Country Western wasn't a particularly well known Gibson flat-top, but I'd had one for a while and thought it would be good to have a cutaway version. Next, we added a specially designed bridge with unusual individual saddles that are tuneable – in other words you can move each bridge 'insert' in order to fine-tune the intonation, which is quite unusual for an acoustic guitar.

Then I decided that if I was having a cutaway I might as well have more frets to get at, so we made it a 23-fret fingerboard. By this time we were really talking about quite a different guitar – and it's a very blonde guitar, very white looking and definitely pretty. As you can see, the fingerboard has 'Steve Howe' inlaid in large letters from the second to the 12th fret, which I think turned out very well and looks absolutely sensational.

The headstock came out of fantasy land. From the outline it seems like a very decorative L5-style headstock, or maybe even 175-like, but it's certainly very broad, and heavily bound. We took the old-style Gibson script, too, and added that L5CES-style flower-pot inlay, a very neat one of those. And while we were at it I put on those enormous machine heads, Grover Imperials, with the big squared-off buttons. I'm pretty mad for them and have them on quite a few of my guitars. I remember seeing Jan Akkerman using them on his Les Paul. So all this adds up to a very distinctive, unusual look to the headstock.

I've really come to like this guitar much, much more lately. I'm coming round to it again. There are some electronics in it which are OK, but acoustically the guitar's maturing very nicely, and it's turning into a very enjoyable guitar. In fact I would put it into the top 25 guitars that I own, not only because of its playability, but in the way it's built and because of its combination of style and good looks.

THE COUNTRY WESTERN

I bought two of these from George Gruhn in 1974 for the proposed guitar shop, but I kept one for myself. It cost me $375. I'd picked up on the Country Western model when I got an album by Chet Atkins called *Down Home* (see right), Chet's playing one on the sleeve. It was the first time that I'd seen him playing anything but a Gretsch, which intrigued me.

So I took to the model, and I think of it as a sort of jumbo version of the 175, partly because the neck feels like that period and size and scale – that indescribable feel – and of course it has the same fingerboard inlays.

It has a very gentle, soft sound to it which I like, and a bit of a buzz on the top string, but I've never wanted it changed, it's actually something I like about the guitar. Its main purpose, historically and recently, has been as the guitar I took on tour to play in my hotel room. That means it's been shipped around the world left, right and centre. It's probably the single most travelled

Custom *(below) I asked Gibson to build me a deluxe version of my Country Western flat-top, but with the bonus of a cutaway. If you compare the body shape to the Country Western further down the page, you'll see how closely they followed the original outline of that little-known* Gibson. *Other than the cutaway, the departures came mainly at the bridge, which is quite an unusual shape, and at the headstock, which is broader than the Country Western's. Another nice touch on this guitar is its abalone binding – I like the way that it makes the guitar glow around the edges.*

On stage *(above) This was taken at a soundcheck on Yes's* Drama *tour of 1980, and I think it may have been intended for use by Gibson to advertise the fact* *that I was using the custom guitar they'd made for me. The picture illustrates rather well how the guitar's fancy inlays illuminate under the stage lights.*

▦ GIBSON COUNTRY WESTERN 1957

Factory order: U2288 20
Country Western produced 1956-1978

Country Western *(above) The history of this model is rather complicated by the fact that various combinations of different names – Southerner Jumbo, SJN, and Country Western – were used by Gibson from the 1950s to the 1970s.*

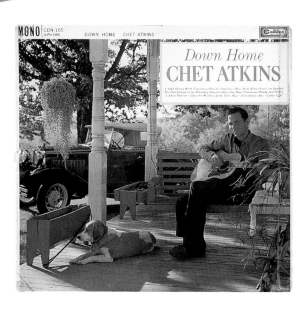

Sleeve *(left) Here's a relaxed looking Chet Atkins sitting on his porch playin' a good old Country Western. And what a car…*

guitar I have, it's been everywhere I've been on all those tours with Yes, Asia, GTR and ABWH. When I think about those years, it was always there – it's only been in more recent years that I've found I don't actually do a lot of playing beside the two- or three-hour concert. That's enough for me, that's what I'm there to do.

Being around on tour so much, of course it's been a writing guitar. From the tours I've got piles and piles of tapes of bits of songs, original ideas, all done on the Country Western. While there's not really any one guitar that I write things on – I tend to move across guitars, bits of tunes and songs get written on various guitars

– I could say that most things that I wrote in the 1970s on the road, which we used to do a lot, were written on that guitar. In a way Yes wrote on the road as a kind of a need, because in a way that's how we kept our road sanity, having something to do together. Or on your own. You were cut off from reality, and writing provided a worthwhile focus.

The Country Western's main recording appearance is on 'Pleasure Stole The Night' from *Beginnings*, quite a dear song to me. It's a very warm song – my wife wrote the words – and I really didn't want to play my Martin 00-18 on it. I'd always wanted to use this Gibson, but it never seemed to fit. Here, it really worked, it's the main rhythm guitar. I also used it on that album to double up the Dobro on the track called 'Ram'.

I always find the Country Western a relaxing guitar to play, in the way that most Gibson jumbos are lovely to play – light, just like a Gibson, where it's made easy for you. It's a very endearing guitar. It's not a great guitar, but it means a lot to me.

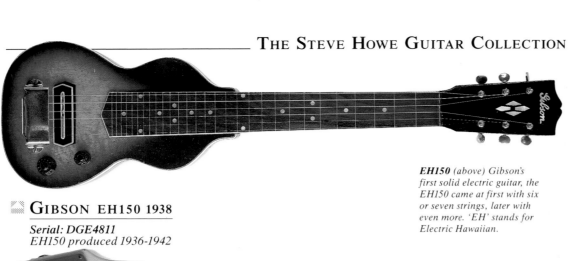

GIBSON EH150 1938

Serial: DGE4811
EH150 produced 1936-1942

EH150 (above) Gibson's first solid electric guitar, the EH150 came at first with six or seven strings, later with even more. 'EH' stands for Electric Hawaiian.

GIBSON BR9 c1953

BR9 produced 1947-1959

BR9 (above) An interesting combination of wooden body and plastic hardware. Note the numbered frets, just in case you get lost as you slide around the strings.

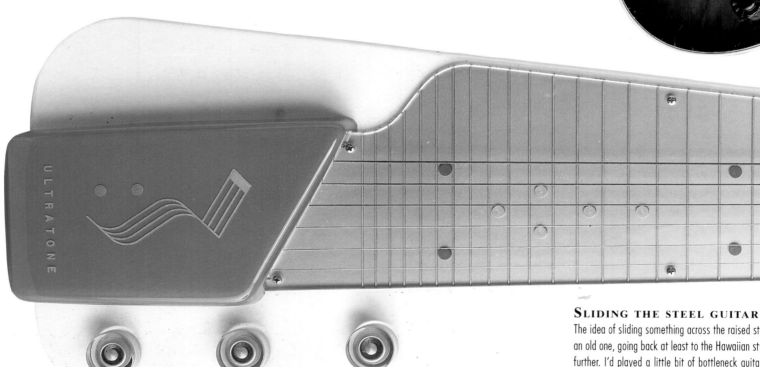

GIBSON ULTRATONE c1949

Ultratone produced 1947-1959

Lap steel (right) This is a Polaroid of me playing the EH150 writing alone at the farmhouse in Devon in the early 1970s. It shows rather well the lovely thick binding on the sides of the EH150's body.

SLIDING THE STEEL GUITAR

The idea of sliding something across the raised strings of a guitar is an old one, going back at least to the Hawaiian style, probably even further. I'd played a little bit of bottleneck guitar before I got into Yes, for example on 'Strawberry Fields Forever' on Tomorrow's album where we had a slide guitar sound, so I probably pulled out a bottleneck for that song. But it wasn't until I got the BR9 steel guitar that I started working with a slide guitar in Yes, and then it really took off: a whole new part of my work.

One thing that is confusing about these kinds of guitars is that there are so many different names associated with them: you can hear the style called lap steel, steel guitar, Hawaiian guitar, slide guitar, bottleneck... and it all comes down to the same basic idea. You have a guitar with a higher action than normal, so that you don't make a noise hitting the frets, and you slide something – a metal bar, a bottleneck, a knife even – across the strings instead of fretting them. It's a great sound!

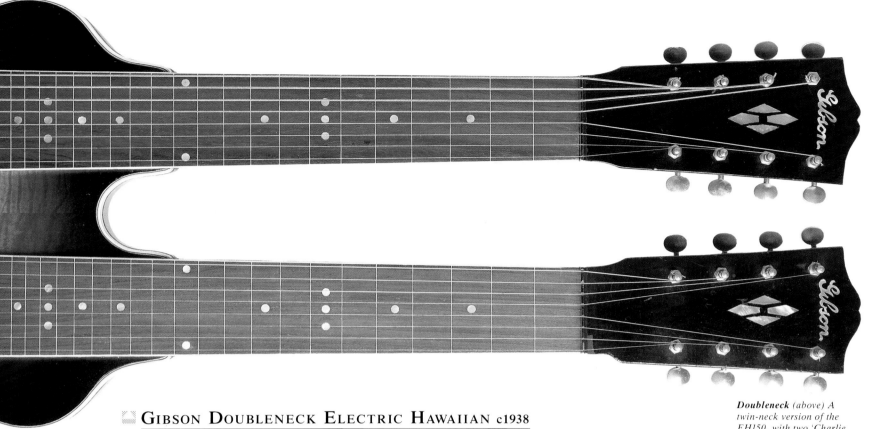

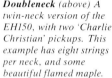

GIBSON DOUBLENECK ELECTRIC HAWAIIAN c1938

Serial: 171-3
Doubleneck Electric Hawaiian produced 1937-1942

Doubleneck (above) A twin-neck version of the EH150, with two 'Charlie Christian' pickups. This example has eight strings per neck, and some beautiful flamed maple.

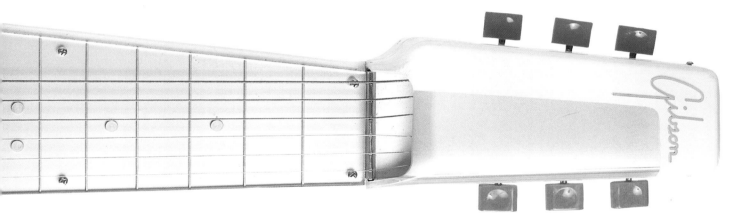

Ultratone (left) An effective use of plastic components combined with its sleekly styled lines give the Ultratone a stunning visual presence. I'm sure it must have seemed wonderfully futuristic when the instrument was first launched by Gibson back in the late 1940s.

AND YOU AND I AND STEEL

The BR9 was my first steel guitar, bought from We Sell Guitars in New York on one of our first US tours in the very early 1970s. I put the guitar to work in Yes quite quickly. It's on *Close To The Edge*, on 'And You And I' and 'Siberian Khatru'.

'And You And I' was the first time I'd used steel on a Yes record, because there was a sound I wanted that I couldn't make on ordinary guitar: a sort of sliding, bending, slippery sound. I play some quite respectable steel on 'Siberian Khatru' too, using an idea that I still like to use today. What you do is to have one steel going up, and just as it starts going up another starts going down. You can't really tell what's happening, and I really like that sensation. Early Yes steel was always the BR9, and on-stage I would have it set up simply on a plain table. But as soon as I got my Fender twin-neck steel that became my favourite (see p40).

I'd always liked the sound of steel players, like Speedy West who made those great records with Jimmy Bryant in the 1950s. And

so when I got the BR9 I seriously began to wonder why on earth I hadn't got into steel guitar years before. At that point I hadn't thought about going on to pedal steel – it just seemed so exciting to be able to slide about all over the place on the lap steel, much more than I could on a guitar. All of a sudden I could do the things that Santo & Johnny used to do on records like 'Sleepwalk'. I love the way that you can be incredibly vague on a steel, just creating a kind of haunting atmosphere in the background.

TWIN NECKS AND EIGHT STRINGS

I bought the single-neck EH150 because of the Charlie Christian pickup. I took it off straight away and stuck it on my Gibson FDH (see p28), because I had other steel guitars. Then I had it all put back and fitted out properly so that all the pots worked, and I had a proper socket put in rather than having the wire hanging out of the side, which is how the EH150 came to me.

But what I really wanted was the twin-neck version, the

Doubleneck Electric Hawaiian, because I'd seen one in a catalogue picture and it looked just amazing. Ed at Silver Strings in St Louis turned up an incredible looking example, and I had to have it, it was such a nice collectable piece. Unfortunately, it's an eight-string and I'm used to six-string laps. But it's a lovely piece of machinery, and I'm pleased to have it in the collection.

The Ultratone came from Pete's Guitars in Minneapolis, and it's a fantastic guitar, a great thing to show off, and certainly the most exquisite looking single lap I have. Unfortunately it got damaged by customs once, they crushed a case that it was in, and consequently some of the Bakelite got damaged (although we've managed to hide it in the picture). I could write another book just on the times that my gear has come back knocked around by customs, and it's been very expensive repairing things. Anyway... the confusing thing about playing the Ultratone is that the fretboard markers are a little more zany than I'd really want. Practical guitars always end up getting used more than lovely things like this.

Headstock *(right) Some of the earliest Gibson instruments had a striking star-and-crescent logo, bu gradually this attractive script-style 'The Gibson' marque began to appear. Sometimes it is used in combination with other decorations, such as the stylish fleur-de-lys seen on this guitar-banjo.*

ES150 *(above) Only the second electric guitar model that Gibson produced, the ES150 was pipped to the post by the EH150 steel which came out a little earlier in 1936.*

GIBSON GUITAR-BANJO c1921

Factory order: 11554-1
Guitar-Banjo produced 1918-1940

Guitar-Banjo *(left) A 1934 Gibson catalogue helpfully described the unusual guitar-banjo as a "beautiful combination of guitar sweetness and banjo brilliancy, with full six-string guitar fingerboard and neck adapted to a regular Gibson banjo rim. Perfect for banjo bands, mandolin orchestras, or in small dance combinations."*

PLAYING GIBSON BASS GUITARS

I'd always had a bass, a Vox (see p66) which was something of an experimental short-scale monster. I'd had this idea that Gibson must make the best basses, and the EBO was the first one I bought. I got it in 1974 from Ed at Silver Strings in St Louis, for $400, and I suppose I wanted to see if I could get the Jack Bruce sound. I've always liked raiding the odds and sods boxes in guitar shops, and so I have an incredible collection of knick-knacks for guitars, and Gibsons in particular. When I used to go to the Gibson factory in Kalamazoo I'd rummage around for all kinds of spares, and once I came out with a beautiful new hook-on Tune-o-matic bass bridge, which I got a friend of mine to put on the EBO, and that made it a much better bass. It sounds great through my Ampeg amp, and it's the only bass I have with a really warm jazz sound – my other basses tend to be a bit twangier.

In the States there are a lot of people in the guitar world who know me, and when I was on tour they would come around to hotels

GIBSON EB6 six-string bass January 1964

Serial: 158750
EB6 produced 1960-1966

EB6 (above) This rare six-string bass, made by Gibson in the 1960s, was tuned an octave below a normal guitar. It produced a wonderfully dark sound.

GIBSON ES150 1939

Serial: EGE6041
ES150 produced 1936-1955

EB0 (below) An example of the first style of EB0, effectively a bass version of the double-cutaway Les Paul Junior guitar. That first type was made between 1959 and 1961. After that it gained an SG-style body, like the EB6 pictured at the top of the page.

GIBSON EB0 BASS c1960

Serial: C12409
EBO produced 1959-1978

and backstage rooms to show me guitars. It was Pete from Pete's Guitars who got me the EB6 six-string bass, probably in about 1978: he rang up to tell me he'd got a couple of really rare things, which he brought along to the hotel. I already had a Danelectro six-string bass (see p68) which I'd used on my first solo record, *Beginnings,* so I already knew that six-string basses made a very useful sound, and suited guitarists.

I recorded with the EB6 on my second solo record, *The Steve Howe Album,* on the track that opens the LP, 'Pennants'. You can hear occasionally that it's quite obviously a six-string bass, the way it plays up high. I also used it on some other tracks on that album, like 'The Continental', where I played it with a drumstick.

That was the only album on which I used the EB6. I was actually looking for a good general bass guitar that I could rely on, and the EB6 wasn't it (see Fender Precision, p44). In the early days of Yes I used to play a bass duet on-stage with Chris Squire, which was good for both of us. It showed a different side of what I did,

and also made me realise that playing bass was something I really wanted to do. I used one of Chris's basses for that, a Fender Telecaster Bass with an extra pickup.

CHARLIE CHRISTIAN'S ELECTRIC
The ES150 was another from Pete's Guitars, bought in 1989. I'd been looking for one for a few years, and I saw this one and was initially disappointed because it's quite beaten up, particularly the scratchplate. I still to this day can't work out how anyone could make a scratchplate look so bad – it almost looks as if someone's been tap-dancing on it. But when I plugged it in and played... yeah! It delivered that lovely old jazz sound.

It has the Charlie Christian pickup, and the two very old knobs look great. The way that the pickup is built into the ES150 pleases me – the fact that it has three horrible screws on it isn't all that nice, but that's how they did it.

It really was a collecting guitar, but I wanted to be able to

make that original sound. Here was a chance to get the Charlie Christian model under my belt, so to speak, and I do like this guitar. You almost hear Charlie Christian touching the strings, it has quite a microscopic, accurate sound, very unstylised and raw. It's the basic electric guitar, functional and without trim.

GUITAR MEETS BANJO
Since the 1970s I'd had the Bacon & Day banjo guitar (see p81), and I thought that was the one. But somewhere in my travels I saw this open-back Gibson with its slightly bent headstock and a much bigger body. The minute I picked it up I thought that's it, the Bacon & Day's history, I liked this softer but bigger sound. I take it down to a lot of sessions – it was there for the ABWH album, for *Union,* my solo sessions – and it gets tried out, but usually it's just too thick and muddy. It has such a highly percussive sound, it's hard to place it in a track. But I like to know I have that colour available to me, and now and again it's going to get called for.

GIBSON SUPER 400CES March 1963

Serial: 61317
Super 400CES produced 1951-current

L5CES (right) Some aspects of Gibson's early 1970s style are evident in this L5CES, such as the logo-stamped pickups, and the 'triangular' shape to the yellow segment of the sunburst finish.

GIBSON L5CESN April 1957

Serial: A25409
L5CES produced 1951-current

Super 400CES *(below) The Super 400CES is Gibson's biggest electric guitar: at 18 inches it's an inch wider than the L5CES. Changes to the 400CES's cutaway followed those of the L5CES. This model has the typical sharp cutaway of the 1960s, called a 'Florentine' cutaway by Gibson.*

On-stage *(left) I've only taken the 400CES on one tour c1975 instead of my 175, so this is quite a rare shot. I wore it a bit lower than usual, because of its large size.*

Wes Montgomery *(below) He symbolises to me much of the greatness of jazz guitar, and since he used an L5CES, those guitars bring back memories of Wes. I was fortunate to see him in London when I was 16 and it made a serious impression on me. He didn't play the way I expected from hearing his records, it was a much more bluesy jazz. He played with this remarkable ease, like a man built for the guitar, never seeming to find anything very difficult. He played* totally across the guitar, and had this ability to hook into a phrase and use the timing of it, which is such a skill. He was quite a perfectionist, too: you don't hear Wes making many mess-ups, he's a very clean player. He used his right thumb a lot for single-line playing, and he had the guitar up loud but actually plays it quietly, which gives such a special sound. To me, the best of Wes Montgomery on record is when he's cooking with a small group.

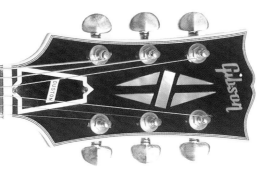

GIBSON L5CES c1971

Serial: 892299
L5CES produced 1951-current

L5CESN *(left) The L5CES was a very successful combination of ideas from Gibson's acoustic L5C and electric ES5 guitars. In the 1950s, L5CESs had this rounded cutaway, called a 'Venetian' by Gibson. The earliest L5CESs came with P90 pickups, but from around 1954 to 1958 they had these 'alnico' pickups with big rectangular polepieces, after which they were given humbuckers. In the 1960s the L5CES came with a sharp cutaway (like the Super 400 up on the left), but the rounded type has been back on the guitar since 1969.*

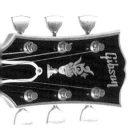

CUTAWAY ELECTRIC SPANISH

I bought the Super 400CES in England, and I remember I didn't like the smell of the guitar at first. I'm quite sensitive to the smell of guitars – after all, they'll be close to you. I've turned down some quite nice guitars because I haven't liked the way they smelt. Sometimes they might smell of lacquer, which means they've been badly resprayed: a guitar should smell only of wood.

I'd seen Elvis Presley playing a Super 400CES on that 1969 'comeback' film. It was actually Scotty Moore's guitar. There's a dreadful moment after three or four songs where Elvis suddenly says, "Give me your guitar, Scotty," takes his Super 400 and strums it for the rest of the show. Scotty sits there looking glum with an acoustic, and as a guitarist I know what he's going through! But that film was a major step for the Super 400, because that was *Elvis Presley* playing it, and it looked seriously good, a sunburst Super 400 against his black suit.

My Super 400CES was beautifully collectable, and a good buy – I've since found out it's one of only 29 sunburst 400CESs made in 1963. It has a fine early Gibson sound, and a marvellous neck. I don't mind the big size – in fact on a big stage a big guitar can work well, whereas a small guitar can seem insignificant.

I bought the blonde L5CESN around 1972 from a private owner in Miami for $650, which I think is one of my best buys. It's one of only 15 made in 1957. It does sum up very nicely a period when there was some great craftsmanship going on at Gibson.

In 1973 Yes went to rehearse for the *Topographic Oceans* LP in the Manticore cinema that ELP were renting in west London. I don't know exactly what it is that happens to me before an album, but I make some decisions about what kind of guitars I might use, and I took the L5CESN down to this month-long rehearsal with the intention of using that guitar on the album. But it turned out that I began to find it unsuitable for what I was doing, especially as it was a little prone to feed back at the levels I was playing at – which weren't incredibly loud. So for *Topographic* I went to the Gibson ES345 again (see p16) and on to the Les Paul Junior (p36), because they suited my purposes much better. The only piece I've recorded on the L5CESN hasn't been released, a version of Wes Montgomery's tune 'Four On Six'.

I bought the 1970s L5CES new from Manny's in New York. When we went to Switzerland in 1976 to make *Going For The One* I took that guitar along. It was quite refreshing, because I wasn't playing an old guitar, and in a way I didn't have to be precious about it. It was just an L5CES – a beautiful looking thing and a nice guitar, but not that important overall.

'Wonderous Stories' on that album has a really big rhythm picture as I strum away on my Portuguese 12-string (see p64). At the end I pick up the L5CES and get into some sweet octaves, and then I blare away a bit: some of it gets rather lost, the single-note runs, but I was really quite pleased with what I did. I had a good time recording it, and once again I wasn't afraid to mix jazz with rock.

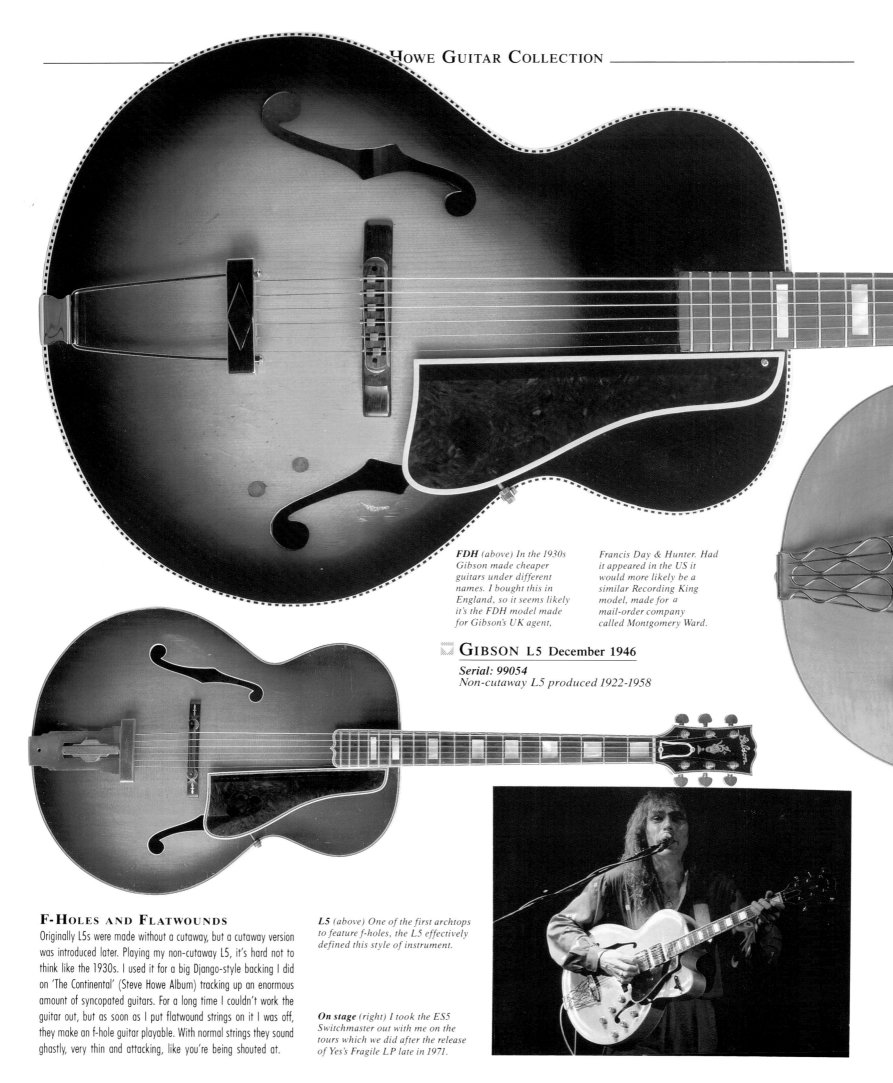

FDH (above) In the 1930s Gibson made cheaper guitars under different names. I bought this in England, so it seems likely it's the FDH model made for Gibson's UK agent, *Francis Day & Hunter. Had it appeared in the US it would more likely be a similar Recording King model, made for a mail-order company called Montgomery Ward.*

GIBSON L5 December 1946

Serial: 99054
Non-cutaway L5 produced 1922-1958

F-HOLES AND FLATWOUNDS

Originally L5s were made without a cutaway, but a cutaway version was introduced later. Playing my non-cutaway L5, it's hard not to think like the 1930s. I used it for a big Django-style backing I did on 'The Continental' (Steve Howe Album) tracking up an enormous amount of syncopated guitars. For a long time I couldn't work the guitar out, but as soon as I put flatwound strings on it I was off, they make an f-hole guitar playable. With normal strings they sound ghastly, very thin and attacking, like you're being shouted at.

L5 (above) One of the first archtops to feature f-holes, the L5 effectively defined this style of instrument.

On stage (right) I took the ES5 Switchmaster out with me on the tours which we did after the release of Yes's Fragile LP late in 1971.

GIBSON FDH c1935

FDH produced c1934-c1942

FDH (below) Changes made over the years include new tuners, fingerboard and inlays, truss-rod, *bridge and tailpiece. Down on the body, filled holes show where controls for a pickup were once positioned.*

Headstock (below) These simple and unusual block inlays are typical of FDH and some Recording King models made by Gibson.

Jamaica I worked with singer Keith West in Tomorrow and on his solo singles like 'Excerpt From A Teenage Opera'. In 1968 we went to Jamaica to write new songs together, taking a guitar each. I took my FDH, but it was damaged en route, which spoiled the *writing idea. Keith's guitar was a cheap Gibson Cromwell, and I'm playing it in Keith's photo (above right). Later I had a long correspondence with the airline (above left) in an effort to get them to pay for the repairs to the damaged FDH.*

GIBSON ES5 SWITCHMASTER November 1959

Serial: A31696
ES5 Switchmaster produced 1955-1962

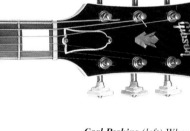

Switchmaster (above) In 1949 the ES5 became the first electric guitar with three pickups. But Gibson had given too little thought to its controls, and six years later brought out the ES5 Switchmaster, its four-position switch offering each pickup or all three.

Carl Perkins (left) When I first saw my Switchmaster it reminded me of Carl Perkins, the great rockabilly player. I'd seen him using one in many pictures. Here, he's playing an early example with P90 pickups; my humbucker version appeared around 1957.

A FRAGILE SOUND

I bought the Switchmaster in 1971 from guitarist Tim Renwick, who was then in a group called Quiver. I started looking after this guitar just like the 175: I carried it with me, nobody played it, nobody touched it. This was my new, precious super-guitar. So when we rehearsed for *Fragile* I used 175 and Switchmaster, choosing between them. And in the studio only 'Heart Of The Sunrise' was played on 175. The rest of *Fragile* is Switchmaster.

'Long Distance Runaround' is a perfect example of what I call the 'gulpy' sound of the Switchmaster with all three pickups on. It's a sound you just can't get with two pickups, and it's different to a Strat's three-pickup sound, somehow more human. Tripling the magnetic poles seems to bring out an individual character in each string, as opposed to a more uniform sound if you use one pickup at a time. Use two, and you start to get qualities in the string, but with three there's this incredible individual string sound.

I carried both guitars on tour, Switchmaster and 175, and

sometimes I'd buy a seat next to me for them. The tours we did straight after *Fragile* were a mixture of headliners and supporting shows. We did strange gigs like Yes supporting ELP... which was a lot of egos at once. The Switchmaster certainly had its moment, a very big moment. The rise of *Fragile*, especially in America, brought Yes into focus: we had a hit single in 'Roundabout', the album was a hit, we were on top of the world, and I was playing the great blonde Switchmaster. It really was a success-story guitar.

BEAUTIFUL F-HOLES

Early in 1965 I bought the FDH in Selmer's shop in Charing Cross Road, London, six months after they'd sold me the 175. I saw it hanging up and it definitely called to me, as I'd not yet found a decent acoustic. The FDH was only £50 so I took it, this curious, huge guitar – it's four inches deep. I liked the fact that it had history, that it was a pre-war guitar. To me that was a big word, 'pre-war'. Wow! That's ancient. I've never found another like it, and

the f-holes seemed the most beautiful Gibson f-holes ever.

Around 1984 I sent it to Gibson and they refinished it to the condition it's shown in above. They cleverly filled in an enormous gaping hole where the front pickup used to be, and you can see two filled holes where the volume and tone were. I think it had a Hofner pickup stuck in it when I bought it, and there was a phase when I had a Charlie Christian pickup in it. But I gave up on that because it has such a deep body that it fed back very badly.

But mainly I remember the FDH as the guitar I sat with at home and wrote lots of tunes on. It was good for finding chords, for improvising on, and I particularly remember writing bits of *Close To The Edge* on it. I gradually found that it settled in, that the sound wasn't harsh like many f-holes are. It's actually quite warm sounding. It's been in studios and been compared to other guitars, but I don't find much call for f-hole guitars on recordings. It has made some appearances, though: when it still had the Hofner pickup, Chris Squire used it to double his bass part on 'Roundabout'.

GIBSON TAL FARLOW May 1963

Serial: 62193
Tal Farlow model produced 1962-1967

Tal Farlow (below) Made in collaboration with jazz guitarist Tal Farlow this striking model (shown here at close to two-thirds actual size) has a scroll near the cutaway recalling flourishes on early Gibson instruments. Otherwise similar to an L5CES, the Tal has a slightly shallower body. This example boasts a superbly figured maple top.

GIBSON BARNEY KESSEL CUSTOM March 1967

Serial: 893202
Barney Kessel model produced 1961-1971

Barney Kessel (above) Gibson teamed up with another notable jazz guitarist to produce an instrument that unusually featured twin cutaways on a 3in-deep body. Parts were gold-plated on this Barney Kessel Custom, nickel-plated on the Regular version.

TALES OF TAL

I bought the Tal (*below*) in 1974 from a dealer in New York for $725. I'd been looking for a Tal Farlow for quite a few years, because it looks unusual and has a nice woody sound. But I wouldn't suggest that you buy a Gibson Tal Farlow in order to sound like Tal Farlow. The reality is that you will sound like yourself, and you won't achieve similarity in sound by playing the same guitar as a famous player. It might lead you closer to him, with a little of the make-up of that sound, but if Tal played any Gibson, any good guitar, I think it would sound reasonably like Tal Farlow.

Tal Farlow's playing hit me like a ton of bricks when I first heard it, and I especially like him in the drummer-less trios. If you can imagine multiple climactic solo ideas, with very exciting melodic and rhythmic content, and all played at high speed, then you've got Tal Farlow. And what Tal does with speed is nothing to do with what a heavy metal player today does with speed. Two completely different things. The most important question you can ask concerning a fast guitarist is this: When does he play slow? If he never plays slow nor uses interesting timings, then please give me a break from him.

GIBSON CHET ATKINS CE c1982

Serial: Pilot 005
Chet Atkins CE produced 1982-current

GIBSON LES PAUL/ROLAND
guitar-synth April 1985

Serial: 81075530
Custom Shop special

INSPIRATION, COLLECTION

The guitarist who was most important to me in my early teens was Frannie Beecher, Bill Haley's guitarist. I also knew Les Paul & Mary Ford's records well – they were almost in my blood. But when I got my first guitar it became clear to me how much I admired Frannie Beecher. He stood next to the singer, and this moody guy with the black Les Paul somehow managed to sum it all up. That was going to be me. I would stand next to a singer and be a singer's guitarist. All Frannie's solos were wonderful little cameos, full of jazzy phrases, and I really wanted to play like that.

There was an incident, very early on, when my 175's jack socket got broken, and while it was being fixed I began to think seriously about the possibility of buying a Les Paul. But then I picked up the repaired 175 and it was like being back in love again. The desire for a Les Paul went away. Much later, I came on to Les Pauls when I was collecting guitars, and I began to build up a very useful range of different versions and types.

Synth live (left) I'm playing the Les Paul/Roland on tour with GTR, some time in 1986. That was my main instrument in GTR, live and on stage, backed up by some old faithfuls like my Telecaster. We did start a second GTR album, with Robert Berry replacing Steve Hackett. Tapes exist, but due to internal problems the project folded.

Synth (above) It has a synth pickup and special controls. It's a good electric guitar, or you can plug it into a keyboard unit and get synthesised sounds.

Les Paul (left) I'm playing with Les at a special Gibson event at Heathrow, England in 1975. He'd signed my Custom before we played.

GIBSON LES PAUL CUSTOM c1956
Serial: 610395
Les Paul Custom produced 1954-current

Custom body (above) My original 1950s Les Paul Custom had two single-coil pickups. But I had an idea for a quadraphonic guitar, and put in four humbuckers. A Custom's normal controls were two volumes and two tones: they became four pickup volumes. I changed the wiring of the old selector switch into an overall tone knob.

Byrdland (below) A short-scale jazz guitar, the Byrdland was apparently designed for Gibson by guitarists Billy Byrd and Hank Garland, hence the name. Along with the ES350T, the Byrdland was in 1955 the first of Gibson's 'thinline' series of guitars.

Despite echoes of the L5CES, the Byrdland's body was around 1½in shallower than existing hollow-body electric models. An unusual variation made in the 1960s had a 'Charlie Christian' pickup unit placed in the neck position.

Hank Garland (left) He was an unusual jazz player, verging toward country and rock. Sadly he had a bad accident in the 1960s that ended his playing career.

GIBSON BYRDLAND March 1978

Serial: 70768023
Byrdland produced 1955-current

Autograph (above) Tal signed this print of my guitar when I met him. He seemed quite flattered that a rock guitarist was so into his playing. I told him that for a long time I wouldn't go anywhere without his Tal album. It has some of his most blistering work, in a great jazz landscape.

SATIN DOLL TO QUEEN

The Barney I bought in Chicago, around 1975. It looked brand new, with tags, and cost about $500. Visually, it's certainly one of the most exciting full-bodies you can be seen with, but I haven't come to play it much. Barney used to pose with the model named after him, but he's usually seen playing a Gibson L7. He was a major influence on me when I was young – the *Pollwinners* album with 'Satin Doll' was the first jazz guitarist's record I had. On that I hear most of what I want to hear about Barney Kessel: tremendous chord work and incredible fluency. But I got sidetracked from him and began to like the more electric sounding players like Kenny Burrell and Wes Montgomery.

I ordered my Byrdland specially from Gibson, because they told me they weren't making blonde versions at the time. The three-quarter scale is nifty and can be fun.

Gibson sent me a prototype of the Chet Atkins CE around 1982 for my reaction. The idea of a solid electric Spanish guitar seemed

somewhat alien, but I instantly went nuts on the Chet, because to have a Spanish guitar that felt like a Gibson was wonderful. I'd had such a mixed life with Spanish guitars, it was hard to settle down with them on tour. But having something like the Chet that you can throw in a flightcase and tour the world with is great – although I'm beginning to pay the cost of that, because the guitar is showing some worrying signs of wear and tear.

The Chet is a live instrument really, and one of its best moments was 'Birthright', live with ABWH (it's probably my Kohno classical on the record). The Chet enabled me to get a dynamic sound that's so hard to get on stage.

But I have recorded with the Chet. With a Spanish or a Martin I was always out in the studio with a mike, but with this it was so enjoyably new to sit in a control room, play acoustic guitar – and actually enjoy the sound. You can hear it on 'From a Place Where Time Runs Slow' on *Turbulence,* and I played Bryan May's Chet when I guested on the title track of Queen's *Innuendo* album.

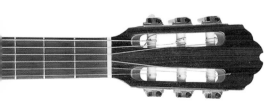

Chet Atkins CE (above) This is a prototype model of Gibson's CE ('Classical Electric'), the world's first electric, solid-bodied classical guitar. The CE first appeared on the market during 1982.

GIBSON THE LES PAUL August 1976

Serial: 26
The Les Paul produced 1976-1979

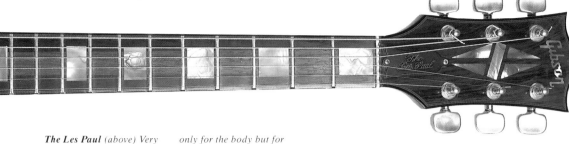

The Les Paul *(above) Very few of these luxurious models were made – mine is only the 26th produced. Gibson's idea was to make an ultra-deluxe Les Paul in limited numbers and at a very high price (around $3000). They used fabulous pieces of flamed maple, not* *only for the body but for more or less everything else that could possibly be made from wood, including the knobs, pickguard, selector ring and pickup surrounds. That luxury attracted me, but more importantly it happens to be a wonderful sounding Les Paul.*

Orchestra *(above) Here I'm recording a session for the tracks 'Double Rondo' and 'Concerto In D' from my 1979 solo record, The Steve* *Howe Album. I'm using The Les Paul through a volume pedal and Big Muff distortion, playing along live with an orchestra.*

Custom *(above) When I met Les Paul in 1975 I took the Custom and asked him to sign the truss-rod cover. He looked at it, and said to me, "Well, I've never seen a Les Paul like this before!" Actually, I think it quite appealed to his way of thinking, because he loves to modify guitars as well.*

On stage *(above) This is the Yes-meets-Buggles band, on-stage for one of our gigs in 1980. Geoff Downes is playing keyboards on my left, Chris Squire's off behind me – and someone has thrown a rose on stage in front of me. On the end* *of that curly lead is The Les Paul. It's one of a handful of guitars I've come across that I somehow seemed to already know from the first moment I played it. I picked it up, and I thought: Ah yes, I can play this any old way I like!*

QUAD AND POWER-CHORDS

The original 1950s Custom cost me $800 from George Gruhn in 1974, and it has a phenomenal neck, probably the best in my collection. I got Sam Li to convert it to four humbuckers. It was going to be my quadraphonic guitar, because I was thinking that we were actually going to have quadraphonic sound. Yes used quadraphonic PAs quite a lot, but never recorded quad. I had a quadraphonic cartridge player in my car at the time, so I thought I'd have a quad guitar – but we ended up putting a mono output on it. I used it on tour with Yes for songs like 'Future Times', and its first recorded use was 'Doors Of Sleep' on *Beginnings*.

Around 1976 Pat Aldworth, Gibson's artist relations manager, told me they were making The Les Paul, and I met the man who did most of the work on them, Richard Schneider. It's undoubtedly the heaviest Les Paul ever! It wasn't a guitar to rehearse or record with all day, unless you could sit down. I didn't like the machine heads on it so I put the chunky Grovers on, but otherwise it's dead right.

I started using it in the studio on 'Don't Kill The Whale' on *Tormato*, and in the 1980s I considered it my best power-chord guitar, so it's on a lot of songs from Asia's 'Heat of the Moment' right through to *Grand Scheme*. The Les Paul gives you total saturation, a really dense humbucker sound. I'm still very happy with what I did on 'Turn Of The Century' from *Going For The One*, where I play sort of spin-repeats after my acoustic Martin section.

SYNTHESISED LES PAUL

The Les Paul/Roland really came into its own when I was doing the GTR project in London, it was my main working guitar for that. GTR was the best experience I've had with guitar synths. The Les Paul/Roland could cover synth work and quite a lot of straight guitar too. I put on a kind of machine head with built-in winders, and I sometimes used to leave the winders opened out on-stage, which looks very weird. I also added a fine-tuning tailpiece: on a synth guitar tuning is even more important than usual.

TV (right) The Junior (one pickup) and Special (two pickups) were budget, slab-bodied Les Paul models, and this second type appeared in 1958 with a double cutaway. Gibson called this version of the Junior, with its yellow-ish body colour, the 'TV Model'.

Studio 1 (left) The guitar area at Mountain Studios in Montreux, Switzerland, in 1977. I'm laying down a part with the Les Paul TV for what was to become Yes's Going For The One album. Behind and to my left are the Fender twin-neck steel and Sho-Bud pedal steel.

TV finish (above) Various theories attempt to explain why Gibson used the name TV for this yellow finish. It's likely that it was aimed to exploit Les Paul's TV series of the 1950s.

GIBSON LES PAUL JUNIOR 1955

Serial: 5 6856
Junior produced 1954-1961, 1986-1991

Junior (above) At first, between 1954 and 1958, the Les Paul Junior and Special models came in this single-cutaway shape, sharing a similar outline to the more expensive Gibson Les Paul models.

Cover (right) Playing the Junior on the Topographic tour around 1974. I'm using a different bridge to the original shown above, in an attempt to overcome the tuning problems I had with the Junior.

GIBSON LES PAUL TV 1959

Serial: 910461
TV produced 1955-1959

TV body (left) *The strange looking things are Bigsby Palm Pedals, which I added. They're called palm pedals because you press them down with the palm of your right hand, which raises the pitch of the B- or G-string. You can add some exciting 'wobbles' to your normal guitar sound. It's almost like a mixed-up steel guitar, a semitone out of tune. Some people dislike the sound, and I've had to fight to get it on record.*

Recording (left) *I didn't keep this 1974 Les Paul Recording long. I used it for the leads on 'Cactus Boogie' on The Steve Howe Album. I quite liked the quality of the low-impedance circuit, but the guitar didn't feel quite right.*

Studio 2 (left) *A session for Drama underway in 1980 at Roundhouse Studios in London. I'm using my 1969 gold-top, another Les Paul that I decided not to keep.*

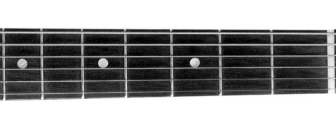

Junior (left) *As usual I've changed the machine heads to workable units. These are chunky Grover Imperials with their distinctive 'squared-off' buttons.*

TOPOGRAPHIC MADNESS

It seemed appropriate that the first Les Paul model I grappled with, the Junior, is the simplest. I got it with the *Topographic* album in mind. Here was a guitar that I couldn't change very much. The tone could be quite useful, at the extremes, and it even worked when I wanted jazz guitar tones. But generally it had a sound: you plug it in, and there it is.

For *Topographic* I ended up playing my 345 on side one and Danelectro 12-string on some of side two, but the Junior is on most of sides two, three and four, where it's the key guitar. Side four in particular is all about the Junior. Of course, it was hard for the guitar to cope with some of the things I wanted to play on it, and I don't think all of it sounds sweet. Looking back, I probably would have chosen to change guitars a little more often. But at the time I stuck with it for continuity and simplicity.

Topographic was a vast recording experience – and madness was going on. There was a point where bathroom tiles were erected

around Jon Anderson to get a reverb he liked. Cardboard and wooden animals were brought in to simulate countryside... so sheep and cows were standing around in Morgan Studios with us. You had to clamber around the studio over all this junk. It was great fun, too, and Jon and I were close collaborators. It was very important to be seen to be winning, to have the right ideas. There was a little unrest from some of the others in Yes about the size of the project. For example, one side was originally 28 minutes long, and we edited it down to 22 to get it on record.

Side three was the most adventurous thing we'd done, we purposefully didn't play in time – the band played one thing and I played across it in a strange way, meeting up at certain places with particular cues. That was good fun on stage, where these intricate arrangements were devilishly hard to play.

I think another notable use of the Junior is on 'Heat of The Moment' on *Asia,* it's the first Les Paul you hear. Then another comes in, and we stacked up various Les Pauls through my old

Gibson Explorer amp, maybe six or seven different takes. Now, I think of this as more evidence that more is not more, that a couple of good guitars are better than six. Near the end of the session we noticed that on one take the guitar was going quiet, so we looked out into the studio and it was full of smoke. We'd actually burned out the Gibson Explorer amp. I thought that was very appropriate for recording a track called 'Heat Of The Moment'.

THE PALM PEDAL CRUSADE

Once I put the Palm Pedals on my TV I was off on a little crusade, because no-one seemed to like the sound. I had to do battle every time I picked it up. You have to be sparing with your wobbles. On 'Only Time Will Tell' from *Asia* I did quite a lot of palm-pedal TV mixed with Telecaster, and I had to fight to keep it there – not in this case because the guys in the band didn't like it, but some record company guy heard it and went crazy about this guitar, he couldn't stand it. So there was a bit of a battle. It stayed.

GIBSON EDS1275 DOUBLE 12
solid October 1964

> **Serial: 70923**
> Solid EDS1275 custom order
> c1962-1968, 1977-current

Live (left) This shot was taken on a Yes tour during the 1970s, and shows me playing the solid EDS1275 six-and-12 twin-neck. I used that guitar on many, many Yes tours, and I took it along primarily for just one song, 'And You And I', where I needed to change quickly from six-string to 12-string. I'd also use it occasionally when we played the song 'Starship Trooper' live.

Solid (left) This solid EDS1275 appeared around 1962, and was still only available to special order. It was the second style of Gibson's twin-neck guitar, a solid-bodied version that looked something like a twin-necked SG guitar. The main change in layout compared to the earlier type (above) concerned the control knobs, all moved to the 'bottom' of the body.

AND YOU AND I AND TWINS

What appealed to me about twin-necks was that they seemed very much in line with what I was trying to do live, where I wanted to move across various guitars in different sections of songs. An easy way of doing that was to have one guitar that was, in fact, two guitars: a twin-neck. It really did work for me, a terrific idea. Of course the disadvantage is that it's one of the most uncomfortable guitars to use, but it's worth putting up with.

I bought the white SG-style twin-neck in a shop in Shaftesbury Avenue in London in summer 1972 for £460. It was the first twin-neck I owned and I used it for years and years, from *Close To The Edge* onwards, for most of the 1970s. I'd bought it specifically to take on tour for playing 'And You And I', to be able to switch six-string and 12-string in that one song. Sometimes I'd play it on 'Starship Trooper' – and I only realised that recently when I happened to see an old video of me playing it.

So the solid twin-neck guitar got hammered. It got broken when

GIBSON EDS1275 DOUBLE 12 hollow c1962

Serial: 90626
Hollow EDS1275 custom order 1958-c1962

Necks Notice how the two necks are slightly angled away from one another, designed to make playing them a little bit easier.

GIBSON EMS1235 DOUBLE MANDOLIN hollow c1962

Serial: 90207
EMS1235 custom order 1958-1968

Hollow (above) "Completely new and exciting," said the Gibson catalogue, "combining the conventional six-string guitar neck with a 12-string neck." This first style of Gibson's six-and-12 EDS1275 had a hollow body and looked to me a bit like a twin-necked version of a 175.

EMS1235 (above) Despite the official Double Mandolin name, the short 'mandolin' neck had six strings, and offered sounds an octave above normal guitar. This one is the earlier hollow-body version; like the six-and-12, it was replaced by Gibson with a solid body version from about 1962.

it was knocked over by a roadie at Manchester Free Trade Hall, and I had it fixed very quickly, inside two days, ready for the next show. I liked the guitar less after that. So later I sent it back to Gibson and they refinished it – and by that time I'd realised that 'And You And I' had to be played on an acoustic 12-string. I don't know why I hadn't realised sooner, but these things happen.

TODD'S HOLLOW BODY

One day I saw a picture of Todd Rundgren playing a Gibson twin-neck, and I realised it was a hollow-bodied twin-neck, not the solid-body type. Now I'd been a real Gibson fan for ages, but I'd never realised until I saw that picture that there was a twin-neck with a hollow body. It looked a bit like a 175 twin-neck to me. So of course I went completely potty, got straight on the phone to George Gruhn that very second and asked him what the hell it was. And George said yes, well, let me see, it's the full-bodied, semi-acoustic twin. I said right, I've got to have one.

George found me one and shipped it over to me. It was a bit beaten up, and since then Roger Giffin has refinished it, put on Grover machines, cleaned all the switches and made the whole guitar gorgeously clean and shiny. It sometimes came into play when I was looking for a different electric 12-string sound, like on 'Australia' from my first solo album, *Beginnings*.

Pete from Pete's Guitars showed up at a Minneapolis gig with the Double Mandolin twin-neck. I asked how much, and bought it straight away. Fantastic guitar! I've used the octave neck occasionally in the studio for doubling up guitar parts, for example near the end of 'Ram' on *Beginnings*. But the six-string part of the guitar is great too, it's got that unusual Bigsby on it, and it really wants to play. It's a big animal, more balanced than the solid six-and-12. This guitar really is burning to get plugged into a Marshall. It's a neat, compact instrument, and it's in fantastic condition. I really do adore the two black twin-necks, they're absolutely gorgeous instruments.

Cover (left) I'm playing my Double Mandolin on this 1975 magazine cover. I think it's a nice touch that Gibson angled the short neck back quite strongly so that the player can see the main neck more easily.

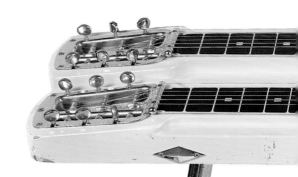

▨ FENDER STUDENT c1954

Serial: 6272
Student produced 1952-1955

Body *(below) Fender
applied a number of
different body shapes to
their lap steels. Compare,*

*for example, the double-
scalloped shape of this
Student with the straight-
edged Champ (opposite).*

Steels *Single-neck models
such as the Student (below)
and the Champ (opposite)
tend to be played on the
player's lap. Steel guitars
with more than one neck,
like this Dual 6 (right) and
the Stringmaster (bottom of
page) are more easily
played on legs. Fender also
made pedal steel guitars.*

Stringmaster *(below) Of
Fender's non-pedal steel
guitars, the Stringmaster
was the model available
with the greatest number of
neck options: it came with
either two, three or four
eight-string necks.*

Student *(above) A renamed version of the
Champion, which Fender
launched in 1949, the
Student was the company's
cheapest lap steel in the
1950s, listing in 1954 at
$59.50, with a finish
described as "mother-o'
pearl plastic".*

▨ FENDER STRINGMASTER four-neck c1953

Serial: 0638
Stringmaster produced 1953-1981

Support *These adjustable
legs enable the player to set
a reasonably comfortable
height whether playing
seated or standing.*

Four necks *I was told by the
dealer who sold me my
Stringmaster (above) that
Leon McAuliff used to own
the instrument. Inside the
case of the Stringmaster was
a scrap of paper noting
Leon's tunings for the four
necks: A6, E13, A6, G11.
McAuliff (1917-1988) joined
the great Western Swing
band Bob Wills' Texas
Playboys as steel guitarist
when only 18, later forming
his own Cimarron Boys
band, and was a very fine
steel guitar player. He had
solo successes with pieces
like 'Faded Love' (featured
on the album pictured
right).*

FENDER GUITARS

Over the next six pages we'll be looking at the Fender guitars in my collection: on this page some steel models, moving to their standard electric guitars on pages 42 to 45.

Leo Fender had opened a radio and record store in Fullerton, California in about 1939, where he met various local musicians who brought in amps for repair. One of these was a violinist and steel player, Doc Kauffman, with whom Leo formed the K&F company in 1945 to make electric lap steel guitars and amps. That didn't last long; by the following year Kauffman was out and Leo had renamed the company Fender Electric Instruments. Gathering around him a team of skilled and clever co-workers, Fender established a growing reputation over the next few years with innovative non-steel guitars, such as the first commercially marketed solidbody electric guitar, the Broadcaster of 1950 (soon renamed Telecaster), the stylish Stratocaster (1954), and the ground-breaking Precision Bass which, appearing in 1951, was another world's first.

■ FENDER DUAL 6 PROFESSIONAL c1957

Serial: 01167
Dual 6 Professional produced 1950-1981

Dual 6 *(left) Fender's first twin-neck steel guitar was the Dual 8 of 1946, similar to this model but with a pair of eight-string necks. The six-string version* *appeared four years later. In 1957 a Dual 6 listed at $199.50, while a four-neck Stringmaster (bottom, opposite page) bore a retail price of $449.50.*

■ FENDER CHAMP c1958

Serial: 00335
Champ produced 1955-1981

Champ *(above) When the Student model (opposite) was dropped in 1955, Fender replaced it with the Champ. This was a similarly budget-priced steel, using a one-piece tuner module that typifies Fender's bolt-together production methods.*

Steel rails *When I first used the Fender Dual 6 steel guitar, around the time of Relayer, it stood on stage and I had to move over to it when necessary. Later, for the Topographic tour, it was on the 'tree' (see p68) but for the Drama tour in 1980 I had it mounted on a clever rail system, so that I could* *move it into position as required. In the pictures above you can see me first of all playing my Telecaster, with the steel out of position (above left). Then, having moved the steel along the rail (above right), it's now right in front of me and situated in a perfect playing position.*

Studio *(above) The Dual 6 has been a constant companion around the world, both live on-stage and in many recording studios.*

SANTO & JOHNNY & BILL

I was using the Gibson BR9 steel before the Dual 6 Professional twin-neck steel, which I bought in the States in October 1973. I've used the Dual 6 all the time since then, on stage and in the studio. It has a great sound, like a bottleneck Telecaster if you want it that raunchy, plus it has a wonderful clean sound.

I came to steel for various reasons. Early on I'd heard records like Santo & Johnny's 'Sleepwalk', the emotive sound of Fender, or the steel player in Bill Haley's band who'd put in that great *jeeee!!* sound on the off-beat. Later, when I started playing guitar I sometimes felt certain things were out of my reach, and the steel guitar suddenly brought them into reach. I've never particularly wanted to play the more absurd things on guitar – all the wailing and screaming – but when I get on my steel that all seems part of the licence. The steel allows that part of me to come out, and my steel work does give me great pleasure. The way you can move about on steel almost defies the way that music is usually supposed to go from note to note or octave to octave. It's like the way people used to use the 'glide' facility on the Minimoog when it first came out. Rick Wakeman did that very well, and I suppose hearing him doing that was another influence on my steel playing.

The two necks on my Dual 6 sound quite different: the first, the closest to you, is thinner sounding; the one furthest away has a thicker, fuller sound. I tend to save that further one for the real icing: if I want it to really *go* then I move to that. I always have the closest neck tuned to E-major, and never with a bass string on the bottom, but an octave of the fourth string. Tuning of the furthest neck varies depending on what I need. Sometimes it's an unusual tuning, or E-minor, or even normal guitar tuning so that I can move to that from guitar without adjusting my thinking.

DUAL 6 ON RECORD

I've used the Dual 6 for many, many recordings. One of the earliest was the gentle, spacey finale of 'Gates of Delirium' (*Relayer*), a section we usually referred to as 'Soon' because that's what Jon is singing most of the time. The title track from *Going For The One* is among the Dual 6's biggest spots – the song is completely played on that guitar. I'm very proud of my work on that track, and it did make quite a change for me to be playing an instrument that was so enveloping for the whole song.

'Into The Lens' on *Drama* turned into a big debate among the group. Everyone was pretty much agreed on all the other songs, but 'Into The Lens' got very tricky at the mix. There were lots of stops on this song, the group was punctuating and I was free to put a steel guitar melody in between. They liked most of what I'd done, but there was one really *dramatic* bit that I called the 'buzzy bee' guitar... and by a group vote it was cut out. I was terribly cross and still am about that not being there.

I've played Dual 6 on my solo records, too. I used it for the melody on 'Break Away From It All' on *Beginnings* and for 'Pennants' on *The Steve Howe Album*. On *Turbulence* it's on 'While Rome's Burning' and 'Running The Human Race', a ballad played on steel guitar with the romantic 'Sleepwalk' approach. 'Maiden Voyage' on *Grand Scheme* has a kind of trade-off between 175 and steel, very melodic, and one of my favourite bits is a very slow steel slide-up on the Dual 6 that lasts about eight beats – it's a really joyous moment which was felt from the heart.

Tele body (above) This design has been around for more than 40 years, and is the classic Fender solid-body electric. I modified this 1950s original by putting a humbucker at the neck position, adding a Gibson-style selector on a new bit of scratchplate, adapting the bridge to six saddles (originals have only three), and changing machine heads and knobs.

James Burton (left) The bearded King of Telecaster, seen here with his employer Rick Nelson in a Fender ad from about 1966. Burton went on to play with Elvis Presley in the 1970s, and has appeared with others including Gram Parsons and Emmylou Harris.

FENDER BROADCASTER 1950

Serial: 0669
Broadcaster produced 1950

Broadcaster (above) During the very earliest production in 1950, Fender's first solid electric was called the Broadcaster, so they're rarely seen today.

The name was soon changed to Telecaster. I've modified my Broadcaster rather a lot: there's a new bridge cut into the body, the tuners are new, and the body's been stripped to natural and bound. I do now regret some of the changes I made, but they were all done to get the guitar feeling right.

FENDER TELECASTER c1955

Serial: 8414
Telecaster produced 1951-current

Telecaster (below) Quite a few players want to make their Teles more ballsy, and the most common remedy is to replace one of the original single-coil pickups (the one at the neck position) with a fatter-sounding humbucker, as I did on this one. Fender reacted to the trend by issuing in 1972 a new model with a humbucker as standard, known as the Telecaster Custom. But I've come to realise that the key to the Tele sound, its real heart, is in the back pickup.

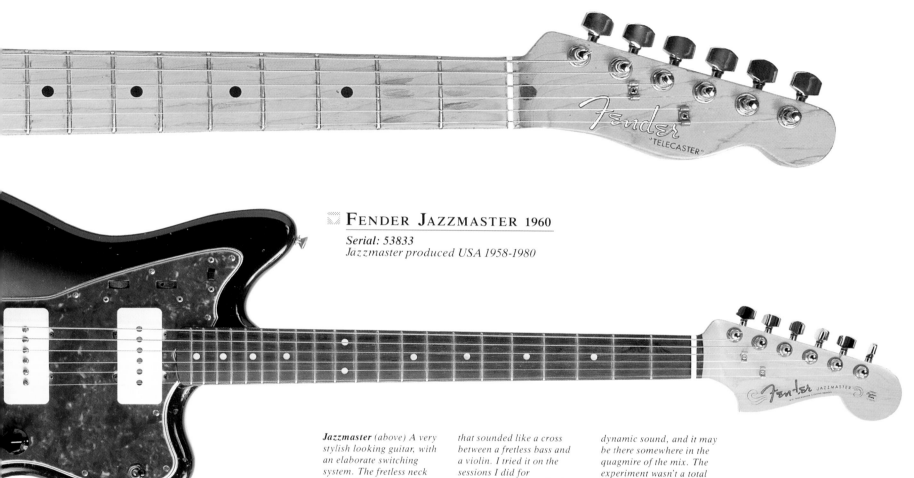

FENDER JAZZMASTER 1960

Serial: 53833
Jazzmaster produced USA 1958-1980

Jazzmaster (above) A very stylish looking guitar, with an elaborate switching system. The fretless neck was made for me by Roger Giffin – I wanted a guitar that sounded like a cross between a fretless bass and a violin. I tried it on the sessions I did for Propaganda's *Secret Wish* album. It's not a very dynamic sound, and it may be there somewhere in the quagmire of the mix. The experiment wasn't a total success, although I do plan to use it again.

PIRATES ON THE TELE

It took a while for me to come around to the Telecaster. I'd enjoyed a couple of important influences early on in my playing career, primarily Johnny Kidd & the Pirates. When Mick Green played his Tele it was like somebody had just knocked on your door, he had a percussive way of playing that was just brilliant. That was my English influence, but the American angle came from James Burton on the Rick Nelson records, a hell-on-earth picking sound.

I got my Tele in 1974 from George Gruhn for $500, and I quickly modified the pickup. *Relayer* was the album where I moved into Fender: 'The Gates of Delirium' was all Telecaster, I don't think there's another guitar in sight on that track. The Tele was great for me then, and although I could make it sound like a Gibson thanks to the humbucker, the back pickup is what makes it a Telecaster. On 'Sound Chaser' I used both pickups together out-of-phase through an Echoplex, with the echo turned up louder than the guitar, and played this strange flamenco-on-a-Tele solo. I used that sound a

lot, like a loud slapback, on *Relayer*. On 'To Be Over' I play a sort of country solo with a true Telecaster chicken-picking sound. I must say that I do like that one, because on reflection it feels just like what I wanted to play.

I've used the Tele since then. On 'Awaken' from *Going For The One* it has a great presence when I open up, playing across lots of moving chords, one of my trickiest solos. 'Release Release' was an important song on *Tormato* where I used Telecaster, a nice sort of chordal approach, harking back to that Mick Green influence again. I thought it was a powerful track, and in a way I would have preferred *Tormato* to have started with that. On *Asia* you mainly hear straight-into-the-amp Tele on the chorus of 'Only Time Will Tell', a hard sound we got at Townhouse studio, which is of course famous for that hard Phil Collins drum sound.

BROADCASTING

I bought my Broadcaster from George Gruhn, and I realised that I

had a pretty historic guitar. But I just couldn't play it – I was used to my Telecaster which was a dream to play. So I wanted to make this guitar the all-powerful Fender, and I took it to Sam Li and got him to modify it – he changed the bridge, bound the body, and put on the Schaller tuners. At the time I had no second thoughts about him doing all this irreversible work. I wasn't really thinking that I'd done anything particularly corrupt, because my style had always been to do what the guitar is telling you to do. But today, I can't say I'm entirely without guilt.

I do like the Broadcaster on 'Pleasure Stole The Night' from *Beginnings*. At one point we only used the reverb send, which gives it a haunting, almost acoustic guitar sound: sometimes I like a guitar that's so distant that it's almost not a guitar. More recently the Broadcaster's been in 'Nashville tuning'. It's like cutting a 12-string set of strings down to six, losing the low-tuned string from each pair. It can give a certain glistening texture to some guitar parts.

FENDER STRATOCASTER American Standard August 1987

Serial: E301671
American Standard produced 1986-current

On stage (left) Live with ABWH and the red Strat in 1989. I had another Strat among my spares – and one night I got fed up and just played my spares. Great fun! Tuning is a problem with Strats, so I did need a spare. Quite often I'd realise the tuning was out, my roadie PJ would run up with the spare, and I'd play that while he was re-tuning the main one again.

WIN STRAT, LOSE STRAT

For some time in the early 1970s I was looking for a Strat that I really liked. I'd borrowed one for a few gigs back in the Syndicats days, but hadn't got on with it. But then I found the sunburst one, probably in 1975, and that was a very good guitar. I first used it on record on *Going For The One,* mainly on 'Parallels'. That track has one of those thoroughbred Yes arrangements: plenty of time changes, guitar breaks all over the place.

On *Drama,* 'Machine Messiah' and 'Tempus Fugit' were pretty much all done on the sunburst Strat, especially 'Tempus' where I was playing it like a lunatic, some very exciting lines: it keeps changing key, stopping, the whammy bar goes mad, and the overall trickiness of the arrangement is quite incredible. I tend to use Strat for that wild side of myself, it's not always a calm guitar.

Unfortunately I lost that original sunburst Strat around the time of GTR, it was stolen along with three other guitars. They caught the thieves, but the guitars were long gone...

Strat (left) When my sunburst Strat got stolen, Fender helped me a lot in my quest to find a decent new Strat, and this red American Standard is the guitar they gave me. It was around the time they gave Jeff Beck his yellow one that he still plays. My red one is excellent, and very stable for a Strat. It became very much the ABWH guitar, but I liked Roland's Strat-style GR so much that when that came along I almost stopped using the Strat. Asia became the GR guitar phase. More recently, I used the red Strat again on my Turbulence album.

Strat *I like the way the Strat projects itself as a guitar with so many possibilities, and I admire Fender for coming up with at least two designs that have withstood years and years of guitar development – quite an achievement. I finally got myself a good Strat in 1975 – this sunburst Strat (below) was one of the best I've come across. As well as putting it to good use in the studio, I played it on-stage with Yes quite a lot in the second half of the 1970s, as shown on the live cover shot from this 1978 magazine (left). I regret to say that it was stolen from me a few years ago.*

FENDER STRATOCASTER c1967

Serial: 165960
Stratocaster produced 1954-current

FENDER BASS VI c1970

Serial: 297969
Bass VI produced 1961-1975

Bass VI *(above) Fender's six-string bass was designed to be tuned an octave below a normal guitar. But I have mine strung and tuned a fifth below, which effectively makes it into a baritone guitar.*

Precision *(right) The world's first electric bass guitar, launched in 1951 and pretty much unchanged since 1957 in the style you see here. This one has a more recent Fender neck replacing the original.*

FENDER PRECISION BASS c1966

Serial: 184109
Precision Bass produced 1951-current

BARITONE SIX

I bought the Bass VI in 1973 for £170, and I soon started to tune it as a sort of baritone guitar, where everything's a fifth lower than normal guitar, using re-gauged strings. It's the same idea as I used on my 335-12 (p16). I found it useful to have it in a register closer to what I was used to, so it wasn't sub-low like a bass. First place I used it was on 'Gates of Delirium' on *Relayer*.

Later, I stuck it into a Marshall and the whole thing came alive – it's like the madman's Stratocaster. I started to use it to double guitar lines, and to play power chords down low. This was around the time of the *ABWH* album, but an awful lot of guitars went astray in the mixing of that, things that were there to give a real guitar picture. However, Jon and some others were used to the keyboard picture that they'd lived with in demo-land. I came along and made this guitar noise right across it – and there were lutes, kotos, mandolins, everything came out of the woodwork. Unfortunately some quite vital things were left out – including some

of the power chords I'd tracked up with the Fender Bass VI.

Later still, on 'While Rome's Burning' from *Turbulence,* I used the Bass VI for counterpoint lines, where I have the band running along with a development of the tune, and then underneath it I've got this medium-register alternate melody going on – and that's what I like to use it for best. It has this ability to interplay with other instruments, but it doesn't clutter up the sound. The whole John Entwistle twang-bassman approach has always appealed to me, and with a six-string bass you can do it all.

I think there is a bit of a gap where a lot more six-string bassists could work, there seems to be some missed potential for that instrument. You can make a lot of noise with it, without taking up much room. That guy from The Shadows, Jet Harris, made a Bass VI sound really good – but what about since then?

NATURAL, PURE, PRECISE

I got my Precision from George Gruhn in 1974, but I soon discovered

a terrible problem with the neck, so I got Sam Li to put a newer Precision neck on it for me, and then I got to like the bass a lot. Some of my bass-playing experience has come from recording myself in my home studio, although a lot of experience before that was based on what I did in big-studio control rooms on my solo albums. Playing bass on my own albums was something I liked doing. I didn't know how to do it, really, other than I knew the root notes, and I heard bass things in my head that I wanted.

With the Precision coming in, I suddenly felt like I had a true instrument, and that this was going to become a friend for life – and that's what's happened. It has a natural purity to its sound that I've never had on any other bass: it doesn't need to be enhanced in the way that some other basses do when you record them. So now it's a matter of: if in doubt, play the Precision. I know that if I start with that I'll be on the right track. I do now get out the Rickenbacker a little bit (p84), but the Precision is the main bass I record with for my solo albums.

SHO-BUD PRO I pedal steel 1974
Serial: 5071

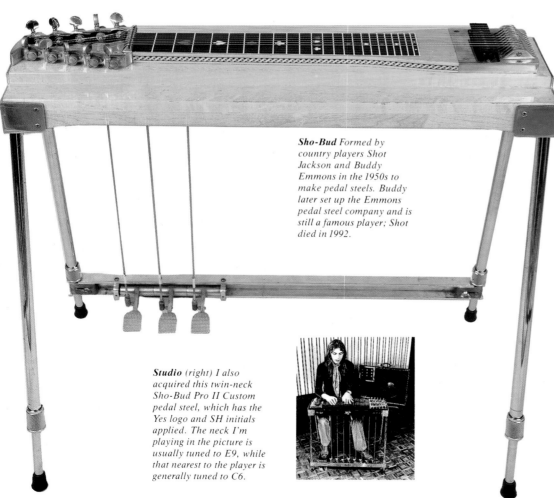

Sho-Bud *Formed by country players Shot Jackson and Buddy Emmons in the 1950s to make pedal steels. Buddy later set up the Emmons pedal steel company and is still a famous player; Shot died in 1992.*

Studio *(right) I also acquired this twin-neck Sho-Bud Pro II Custom pedal steel, which has the Yes logo and SH initials applied. The neck I'm playing in the picture is usually tuned to E9, while that nearest to the player is generally tuned to C6.*

Sleeve *(above) I first heard pedal steel ace Speedy West, an early influence, with Jimmy Bryant on Tennessee Ernie Ford's records.*

RINGING STRINGS

Once I got into steel guitar, I realised that most of the steel I had been hearing was actually pedal steel, and I began to think about getting into that side of it too. On record I was hearing great players like Buddy Emmons and Lloyd Green, and then another step came when we toured with Poco and The Eagles in the early 1970s. I used to watch Poco's pedal steel player Rusty Young and think how good it would be to play that instrument too.

When I was on an American tour with Yes in summer 1974 we stopped off at Cincinnati to visit the Gretsch factory, and at this time Gretsch had a connection with Sho-Bud, one of the best pedal steel makers. I left with the Pro I and got straight into it, finding out how the thing worked. I'd set it up in hotel rooms on the rest of the tour, and make horrible noises for hours!

It fell into place quickly. The pedals alter the strings' pitch, and the way you have to think about playing pedal steel is quite different from guitar. Because you have strings that are tones and

DOBRO NO. 65 1932
Serial: 5498

History Many guitar players of the 1920s and 1930s were seeking extra volume from their instruments, and some found a solution in the resonator guitars made by National and Dobro. A resonating metal cone (or cones) inside the guitar's body produced a loud, brash sound that was much exploited by early bluesmen. Versions with special necks and high action were widely played in Hawaiian music. National and Dobro's history is confusing, to say the least. From 1926 the five Dopyera brothers, Czech immigrants to California, combined, split and regrouped in various combinations to form a number of guitar-producing companies. They also licensed others such as Chicago-based Regal to make resonator guitars. Today, Original Musical Instruments and National Resophonic Guitars continue to produce National and Dobro-style instruments.

Reso-phonic (right) A short- scale, semi-solid, cutaway resonator guitar, made with the National brand by Valco.

NATIONAL RESO-PHONIC c1961
Serial: T62281
Reso-phonic produced 1956-c1964

DOBRO c1933
Possibly Regal-Dobro No. 37

Dobro (above) My two Dobros are set up for different kinds of playing. The black-wood model here has normal string-height and I play it as a regular guitar, while the scroll-decorated model (above, left) has a higher action for slide playing.

---

sometimes semi-tones apart, you have to work more on string-to-string ideas, leaving individual strings ringing. You have to think ahead, about what's going to happen when the pedals come off, for example, and what effect the ringing strings will have.

STUDIO PEDAL STEEL
On record, I first used the Sho-Bud on 'To Be Over' from *Relayer*. It has what I think is one of Yes's most powerful middle sections ever. I had a tune that I wanted to use after the middle eight, but I didn't want to play a normal guitar part. So I figured that the pedal steel might work... and it did. It was great exploring that on the pedal steel, and also it made me realise that once I know a tune, I can play it on pedal steel or anything.

I used pedal steel on the opening of 'Awaken' on the next album, *Going For The One*, and instead of giving it some nice reverb and letting it sit back in the track, we put a flange-type effect on it which gives it an almost watery atmosphere. I got a kick out of

that, because pedal steel usually sounds like a pedal steel. To use an effect on it brought it into Yes a bit more. The Sho-Bud also returns at the end, back to something minimal and sparse after the big arrangement. Sometimes I play regular melodic parts on the Sho-Bud, as on 'Will O' The Wisp' (*Beginnings*). The Sho-Bud is the first thing you hear in the electric section, playing a nice tune, and I like that piece a lot, one of my favourites on the album.

When I did the *Union* tour I wanted to use my imagination in playing the 1980s Yes music I didn't know: from when I wasn't in the band and where Trevor Rabin would be playing guitar parts. I could either play rhythm, which I was only going to do a little of, or – and this seemed a strong alternative – I could drop in pedal steel here and there as a surprise. It made things sound different, and I'd play it where nobody expected me to. Those moments proved to me that I wanted to keep up my work on pedal steel. So it turns up on more recent projects, such as 'Running The Human Race' on *Turbulence* and 'Blinded By Science' on *Grand Scheme*.

ACOUSTIC REALITY
I'd heard Dobros on blues albums and was attracted by their tinny 'street' sound. I got the black-wood guitar-action Dobro around 1974, and first used it on 'Ram' from *Beginnings*. We had some technical problems with the timing, and the guitar had poor intonation, so I recorded the track in sections. Some of the album was made with mobile equipment at our house in London, the gear in the garage and me playing in the kitchen. Atlantic Records paid for a promo film for *Beginnings* that included 'Ram', and that was fun because it showed all the instruments I used.

I got the 'flowery' slide-action Dobro later, and I like it a lot now. I used it first on a session I did for Frankie Goes To Hollywood's *Welcome To The Pleasure Dome* album, and later I used it on my *Turbulence* and *Grand Scheme* albums. My acoustic requirements have grown recently, and my general thinking now is that if I want a sense of reality in the music I play acoustic instruments, and if I want an element of fantasy then I use electrics.

Stepp body (right) Clearly this instrument was designed not only to perform in a new way, but to look very different as well. The control panel on the body governs the storage, recall and modification of pre-programmed and user-programmable sounds.

STEPP DG1 digital guitar c1987

Serial: 7010062
DG1 produced 1986-1988

ROLAND G505 guitar synthesiser c1981

Serial: 100496
G505 produced 1980-1985

Ibanez (right) I'm featured in this 1986 promotional ad/poster for a shortlived MIDI electronic guitar system that was made by the Japanese company Ibanez.

Controls (above) Viewed in this position, the Roland's top row of controls govern: vibrato; guitar-sound/synth-sound/both; two synth tones; master volume. The lower two controls are for balance of synth/guitar sounds and guitar tone. The synthesiser pickup is the thin black unit next to the bridge, while the Strat-style white pickups are for guitar sounds. The instrument came with a 'blue box' GR300 control unit, situated at the player's feet, with facilities for supplying the shape and make-up of the synthesiser sounds – which alas could not be stored and recalled.

SIX-STRING SYNTHS

There really is a terrible negativity from guitarists about synth guitar, and I've shared that negativity. I've been in studios where I've taken in a guitar synth and just had to laugh at how bad it sounded. We'd go through the motions of plugging it all in and setting it up, start to look for a sound... and get nowhere.

Guitar synths first came in during the mid 1970s, and the idea was that you could play a guitar plugged into another unit or two that enabled you to get synthesiser-type sounds. The theory was fine, but in practice the instruments didn't always perform well and the sounds sometimes left a lot to be desired. I think it's a mistake to use guitar synthesis with other things; the sounds can actually be more effective on their own.

My very first experience with guitar synthesis had been an unhappy one. In summer 1975 I bought a system made by Walter E Sear of New York who had developed a very early guitar synthesiser. Basically, it never lived up to the claims made for it, and

cost me an absolute fortune. After being shipped back for modifications at the end of 1976 it became lost in transit and was never seen again.

The Roland, which I got around 1981, was a different story. It was a very good guitar in itself, so I liked to play it not only for synth sounds but for ordinary guitar sounds too. At the time the Roland seemed to be the greatest thing that had happened, enabling me to get a lot of new sounds playing the guitar. Early Asia was very much the Roland guitar phase, and it's on the *Asia* album of 1982, especially the solo on 'Here Comes That Feeling'.

I never really got on with the Stepp, and the Ibanez I didn't like as much as the Roland, although I only had it three months before it was stolen. I've still got the Ibanez controlling rack unit which can be used with some other synth guitars. The silly person who bought my stolen Ibanez is without that rack, which makes it rather useless. I like to use the Roland through the Ibanez rack, and on the GTR tour I used it effectively with the Les Paul/Roland (p34).

Stepp (above) The DG1 came with an 'LSU' control unit (not shown) which doubled as a guitar stand and contained the main synthesiser circuits and interfaces. The British Stepp company spent four years developing the DG1, and later introduced the DGX which was designed as less of a stand-alone instrument and more of a MIDI controller which one could link with other synthesiser units.

Roland (below) The second generation of Roland guitar synths came Fender-styled, as this example, or Gibson-styled. Players did not take to the apparent complexity.

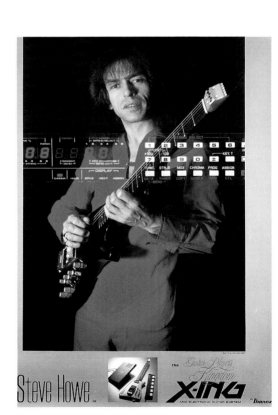

Steve Howe in the Guitar Players Kingdom
X-ING ™Ibanez

Effects (right) I got all the effects virtually the day they came out, from the wah-wah onwards. It was my must-have period. This shot was taken in my storage room in the early 1980s and shows a good selection.

Amplifiers (below) Here's a group photo of some of my Gibson amps taken during the 1980s. In the back row, left to right, you can see: a Discoverer, Lab Series and Les Paul. In the middle row: Explorer, Multi-Stereo, and another Explorer. In the front row: Gibsonette, BR9 (designed to go with the BR9 lap steel, p22), and lastly the EH150 (which was meant to partner the ES150, p24, or EH150, p23).

AMPS CHRONOLOGY

My first amp was a Guyatone that came with that guitar (p66), and then I had a Watkins Dominator for a while, but soon I decided to get a Fender Tremolux to partner my 175 for The In Crowd. Vox came along quite rapidly: in 1966 I went from the Tremolux to using a valve AC50, and that was the best amp I've ever had for the 175. Then I made the worst decision of my amplification life and traded the AC50 for a transistor AC100, which let me down night after night with Tomorrow, blowing up, crackling and always going wrong.

When Yes came along they told me there was £10,000 to spend on gear, so I'd get a new amp – but that didn't happen for a while. Before we recorded *Fragile* we went out and bought loads of Fender Dual Showman set-ups, an unusual choice at the time. Across the back of the stage there would be this wall of Dual Showmans. I had a Binson echo unit on top of mine and a bit of a pedalboard on the floor. After *Fragile* I started using steel guitars, so for those I got a Fender Super Reverb, a kind of Twin Reverb with four speakers. Things went on like that for years. When we moved to the round stage for the 1978-1980 tours I had to get a smaller set-up, so I switched to two Fender Twin Reverbs connected to two extension speaker cabinets.

When Asia started up I went back to two Dual Showmans. For the second tour I decided to have four, and had four 'fake' cabinets built, but I couldn't get them to sound right. There was only one solution: I went back to Twin Reverbs. I still use them, though sometimes when I go to the studio today I take a Twin and a Showman. I also use Marshalls, but I can't get on with them on-stage, and I've got a selection of Gibsons which I like very much (see group photograph above).

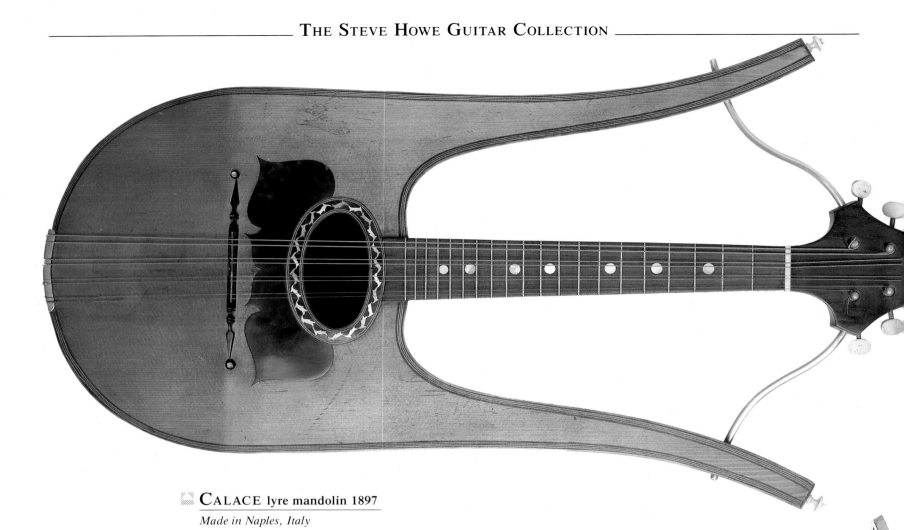

CALACE lyre mandolin 1897

Made in Naples, Italy

Amalie *(above) A print from around 1800 shows the kind of wealthy woman at whom the voguish lyre guitars were targeted. Despite the artist's rendition of a five-string instrument here, most had six strings.*

The Light Guitar

'Light Guitar' *(left) A number of prints and illustrations from around the dawn of the 19th century illustrate the wide popularity of the lyre guitar and related instruments, including this rather fanciful version.*

Calace *(above) It was not only the six-string guitar which received the lyre treatment. This Italian instrument, made some time after the main burst of lyre popularity, has four-course mandolin tuning in a small lyre-type body. It was made by Italian brothers Raffaele*

and Nicolas Calace, who produced guitars and mandolins. Raffaele, whose son Giuseppe became a violin and guitar maker, was also a composer. He died in 1934. Nicolas emigrated to the USA in 1898, a year after this mandolin was made, and died in 1914.

NEO-CLASSICAL HYBRIDS

Lyre guitars are a fascinating type of instrument, first made at the end of the 18th century and into the early 1800s. I began collecting them as soon as I discovered them in the 1970s, drawn to their elegant shapes and often beautiful decorative work.

The lyre itself was an ancient instrument dating back to 3000 BC, having a soundbox with two projecting arms, the strings stretched from the soundbox to a cross-bar or 'yoke'. A so-called 'classical revival' in Europe toward the end of the 18th century led to a vogue for all things considered classical, including hybrids of guitar and harp (harp guitar), and guitar and lyre (lyre guitar).

The first written evidence of the lyre guitar came in a French pamphlet of 1780, although the earliest surviving instrument with a date was made in 1785. Most of the lyre guitars that one sees today were made between 1805 and 1810, when the popularity was clearly at its greatest, and very many were made in France. They were small instruments, mostly played by ladies.

The Roudhloff 'shield' lyre guitar (right) was the first example that I bought, and this like most of the items in this section of my collection came from a musical instrument dealer based in north-west London, Tony Bingham. He also managed to track down the attractive contemporary pictures shown over these pages, and I think they certainly add a great deal of extra interest to a collection of this kind.

Some of the instruments do not possess arms or cross-bars and these are usually referred to as 'yokeless' lyre guitars. The similarity remains in their shape and style, including the fact that most have a base at the bottom of the body on which to stand the guitars upright for display purposes, as we have done here.

Most lyre guitars were fitted with six single strings, at a time when many guitar makers were still using five courses of doubled strings. It seems that the great popularity of the lyre guitar influenced the general change from five doubled courses to six single strings on normal guitars around 1800.

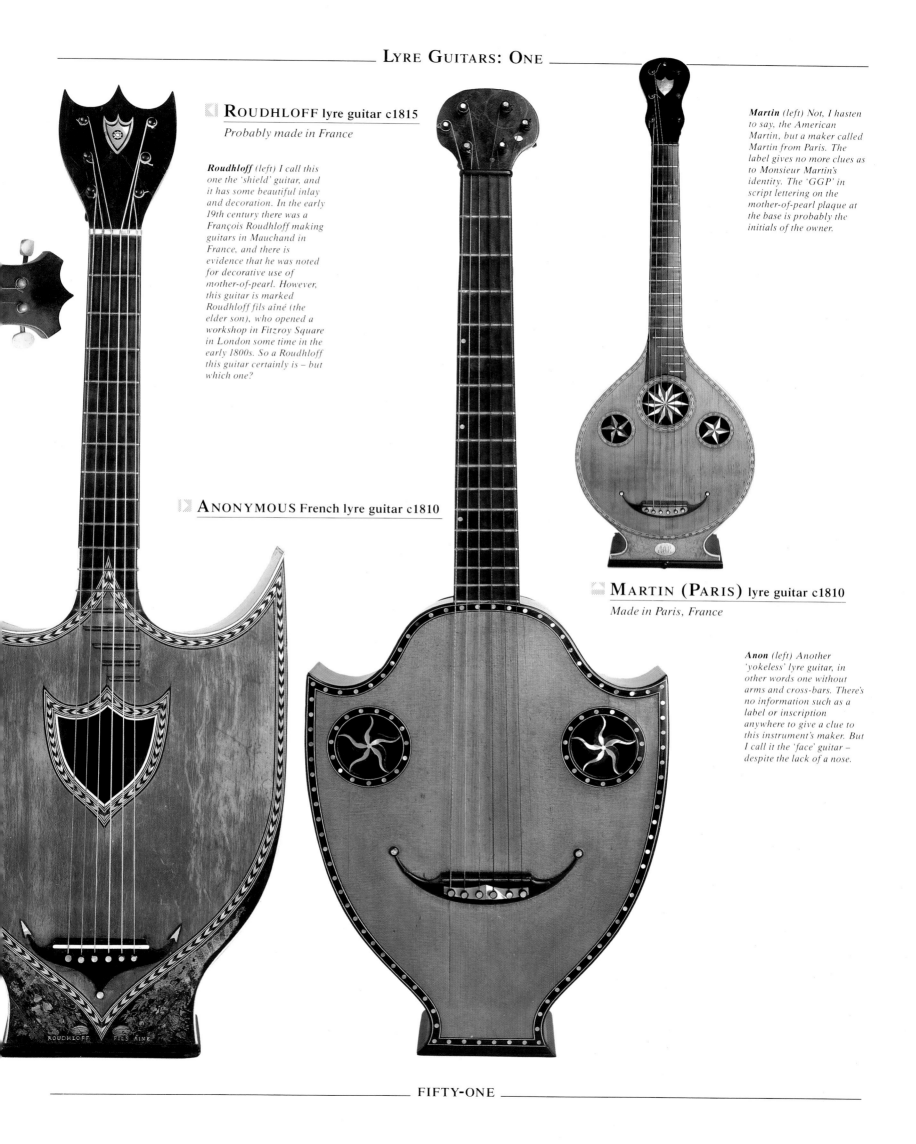

ROUDHLOFF lyre guitar c1815

Probably made in France

Roudhloff *(left)* I call this one the 'shield' guitar, and it has some beautiful inlay and decoration. In the early 19th century there was a François Roudhloff making guitars in Mauchand in France, and there is evidence that he was noted for decorative use of mother-of-pearl. However, this guitar is marked Roudhloff fils aîné (the elder son), who opened a workshop in Fitzroy Square in London some time in the early 1800s. So a Roudhloff this guitar certainly is – but which one?

ANONYMOUS French lyre guitar c1810

Martin *(left)* Not, I hasten to say, the American Martin, but a maker called Martin from Paris. The label gives no more clues as to Monsieur Martin's identity. The 'GGP' in script lettering on the mother-of-pearl plaque at the base is probably the initials of the owner.

MARTIN (PARIS) lyre guitar c1810

Made in Paris, France

Anon *(left)* Another 'yokeless' lyre guitar, in other words one without arms and cross-bars. There's no information such as a label or inscription anywhere to give a clue to this instrument's maker. But I call it the 'face' guitar – despite the lack of a nose.

ROBERT WORNUM lyre guitar c1810

Made in London, England

Lyre guitars *Robert Wornum had workshops in Wigmore Street in London where he made the stunning lyre guitar (right), seen also in a contemporary painting (above). Le Jeune was a Parisian maker of violins and guitars, and his lyre guitar (below) has an unusual soundhole in the shape of a half-moon.*

LE JEUNE lyre guitar c1810

Made in Paris, France

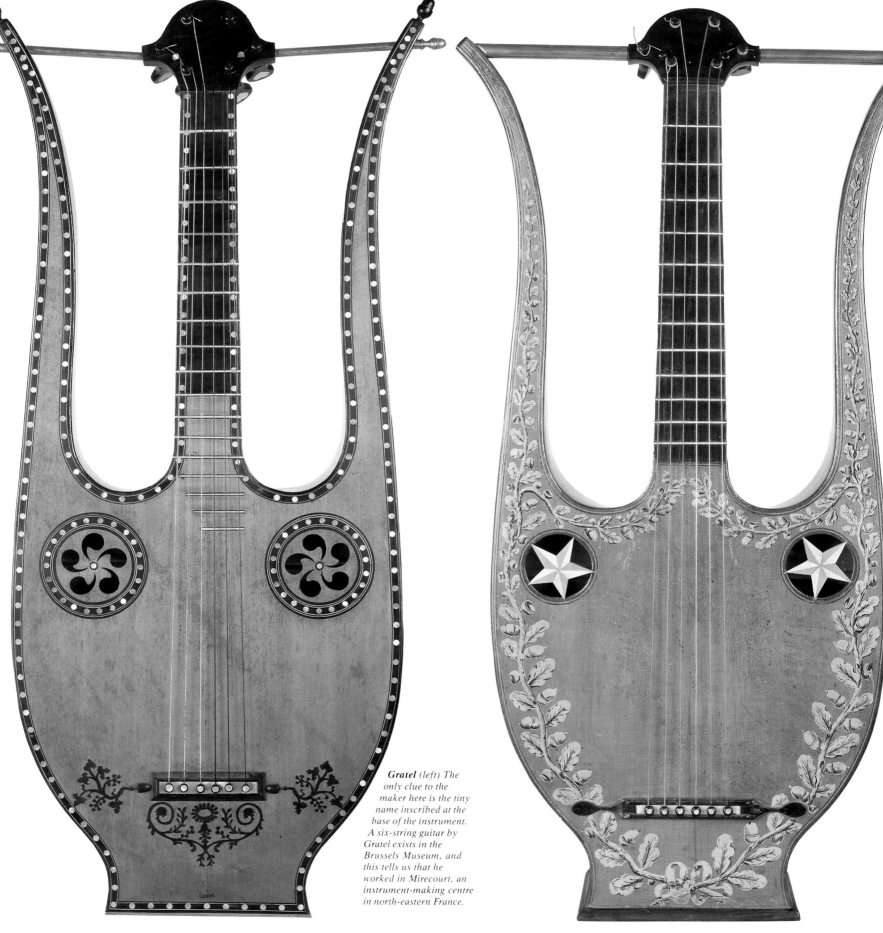

GRATEL lyre guitar c1810
Made in Mirecourt, France

ANONYMOUS French lyre guitar c1810

Gratel (left) The
only clue to the
maker here is the tiny
name inscribed at the
base of the instrument.
A six-string guitar by
Gratel exists in the
Brussels Museum, and
this tells us that he
worked in Mirecourt, an
instrument-making centre
in north-eastern France.

GEORGES WARNECKE guitar c1840

Made in Nancy, France

JEAN-FRANCOIS SALOMON harpo-lyre c1830

Made in Besançon, France

Warnecke (above) You might be surprised that a guitar some 150 years old should have such a modern looking double-cutaway body, but at this time French makers were renowned for producing odd-shaped guitars alongside their more traditional fare.

Salomon (right) This peculiar three-necked instrument isn't a guitar at all – not according to the inventor that is. He called it a 'harpo-lyre', designed to be a cross between a harp and a lyre.

Panormo neck (below) A noted feature of Panormo's guitars was their fine ebony fingerboards which, unlike the flatter boards common at the time, were slightly radiused. For players used to modern guitars this can feel pleasantly familiar.

Panormo (above) Louis Panormo's father, Vincenzo, was an Italian violin maker who worked in Paris and London. When Louis started making guitars in London in the early 19th century, his superb instruments reflected these diverse influences, and part of his guitars' excellence results from a mix of some of the best elements of guitars of the time. Note, for example, the modern-style metal geared machine heads, far superior to the simple peg type tuners that many makers were still using then.

'Sound unit' (left) This print from the late 1820s shows an idea for an early amplifying device. The scheme was patented by Salomon, whose three-necked harpo-lyre can be seen connected to the 'sound unit'. The patent says the link from harpo-lyre to unit is made with two special 'bars'. These support the instrument in a playing position and transmit the vibrations of the instrument to the unit, "producing at least twice the sound of ordinary guitars, and a very satisfying harmony".

Panormo body (below)
Louis Panormo offered a
range of guitars which I
believe were sold for
between two and 15
guineas. I'm sure that this
one would have been in the
top half of that bracket,
considering the level of
attractive inlay that can be
seen in the soundhole ring,
on the bridge, and around
the edge of the top.

COLLECTING ANTIQUE GUITARS

During the 1970s, as my guitar collection began to grow, I started to become interested in the history of the guitar before the beginning of this century. It's actually a lot harder – and more expensive – to collect these early guitars because there are relatively few surviving examples. Many of the instruments I bought came from a specialist dealer called Tony Bingham, who's based in north-west London. He would hunt for the kind of antique guitars that he thought I would like, and you can see many of the catches he made for me over the next few pages.

LOUIS PANORMO guitar 1836

Serial: 9430
Made in London, England

ANONYMOUS French lyre guitar c1810

Various I call the two anonymous lyre guitars the 'gold leaf' (far left) and the 'eagle heads' (left), after their decorations. The harp guitar (below) was the less common type of neo-classical hybrid made in the early 1800s. Josef Laurent

Mast was born in Mirecourt, the son of a violin maker. He was apprenticed to one of the town's most prolific luthiers, Didier Nicolas, and set up his own workshop in Paris during the early 1800s.

JOSEF LAURENT MAST harp guitar 1827
Made in Toulouse, France

Preston and Light (right)
The Preston cittern is seen here in front of a dital harp made by Edward Light in England in the 1810s. The dital harp was an unusual cross of lute and harp with keys or 'ditals' to alter the instrument's tuning.

Preston (above) John Preston was a leading maker of so-called 'English guitars', which in fact were not guitars but citterns.

This one has Preston's patented tuning system at the head that uses string 'hooks' operated by a separate key.

ANONYMOUS French guitar c1835

Imported to Britain by Ferdinand Pelzer

JOHN PRESTON cittern c1775

Made in London, England

French guitar (above)
This was another of Tony Bingham's finds. He told me that it is likely to be one of the French guitars imported to Britain by guitar teacher and author Ferdinand Pelzer. He was the father of the leading figure in guitar teaching in Victorian Britain, Catharina Pratten (see page 59).

HISTORY VERSUS PLAYABILITY

Unlike the bulk of my collection, most of these antique guitars were bought for their historical and/or aesthetic interest rather than playability. The exception is the Panormo: not only is it beautiful to look at and fascinating historically (the label tells you that Panormo's workshop at the time was at "46 High Street, Bloomsbury"), but it's a great guitar to play.

I've seen other Panormos, and rarely have I seen a better one for sale. It plays in a way that overcomes any bias you might have toward the fact that this is an old guitar. As far as I know it's had nothing done to it, too. A lot of Panormo's guitars are still apparently that good – they don't seem to wear out very easily.

And I think it's a beautifully designed guitar, especially the headstock. Panormo advertised the fact that he made guitars "in the Spanish style", and his instruments are considered by some to be particularly reminiscent of the guitars made by the renowned Spanish maker Pagés. I must say that the Panormo is quite

definitely the sort of guitar that you can't help but fall in love with, and it plays every bit as well as my classical guitars, the Kohno and the Ramirez (see p60).

The Preston cittern is also one of the more exotic looking examples I've seen, with very impressive fingerboard and soundhole decoration. I seriously wanted to play the cittern, but after this instrument was restored I couldn't play it because we decided it was too fragile to take the strain of strings tuned to pitch. So it remains an attractive piece.

THREE-NECKED SALOMON

The Warnecke and the Pelzer I wanted simply because they attracted me, but the three-neck Salomon harpo-lyre was something else entirely. I remember Tony Bingham called me when the instrument came in and he said to me, "I've got something special here!" And what a wonderful thing it is. I had to have it. There was a fair amount of renovation that needed doing – I remember there were pegs missing and some

structural damage – and so of course that had to be added into the price. But even though the Salomon was expensive I think it was well worth the outlay.

Subsequently Tony Bingham found the picture of the man sitting playing the guitar plugged into a device that I suppose today we would call an amplifier – but of course it certainly wasn't electric. You can see the picture over to the left, and this made the instrument even more interesting to me. Tony also gave me a copy of the 1829 patent that explains the unit, and this also tells you about the ideas behind the three necks. According to Monsieur Salomon, the middle six-string neck is supposed to be tuned as an ordinary guitar, the seven-string neck (on the left) should be tuned in semitones from low A to high D-sharp, and the eight-string neck (on the right) has to be tuned to a diatonic C scale. Quite a handful, in fact. And of course all in all the Salomon is a huge, unmanageable guitar, and I really can't do anything with it. But it's quite enough for this instrument just to be there.

◧ ANGLO-NEAPOLITAN
guitar-mandolin c1910
Made in England

Morlot *(right) It has all the delicacy of early 19th century French guitar making. The figure-of-eight headstock mirrors the body shape and was common, as was the pin bridge, although the tradition of fixing frets directly into the body beyond the short fingerboard had almost died out. The ebony and pearl binding is magnificent; it's astounding how well preserved it is some 170 years later.*

Mrs Pratten *(below) Catharina Pelzer, one of the leading guitar players in Victorian Britain, married a flautist, Robert Sidney Pratten, in 1854. Mrs Pratten's patron, Lady John Somerset, helped Catharina begin a teaching career in London, at which she seems to have been equally successful.*

Back *(above) We're just showing a back view because the charming decoration is the reason I bought this guitar-mandolin – it has no musical aspect for me. Little is known of Anglo-Neapolitan, although there's a label in the body quoting a patent number that turns out to be for the shape of the body. The patent was granted to a Mr Glaesel in January 1902.*

THE BAMBINA GUITAR

A fledgling guitarist receiving lessons from a teacher today will often also receive some advice on what to look for when buying an instrument. Some teachers go further and will supply suitable guitars to pupils – and a couple of the guitars in my collection seem to show that this is not a new development.

The French guitar on page 57 was one of a number imported to Britain in the 1830s by a well-known guitarist, Ferdinand Pelzer. His daughter Catharina (1821-1895) was a child prodigy and soon began to teach as well as play the guitar. The Bambina or 'baby' guitar – seen in its case (*right*) and in more detail (*far right*) – was designed by Catharina as an easy-to-play first instrument; it too was probably made in France and specially imported.

Catharina also produced a number of popular tutor books for the guitar (under her married name, Pratten). One, *Learning The Guitar Simplified,* was touted as being "used by Her Royal Highness the Princess Louise and Her Royal Highness the Princess Beatrice".

ANONYMOUS five-course guitar c1780
Made in France

Five-course (above) This is the earliest guitar in my collection and as such has for me a certain mystery about it. Certainly there are no marks or labels on it to give a clue as to its origin. Tony Bingham, who sold it to me, says it's almost certainly French.

FIVE TO SIX

There was a revival of interest in the guitar during the late 18th century, and major changes to its construction began to occur. Since the mid-16th century the guitar had generally been made with five 'courses' of strings. ('Course' usually refers to a double string, but is actually a correct term for single, double, or even triple strings grouped closely together.) In Spain in the 1770s and 1780s, and slightly later in other guitar-making countries, there was a move from five to six courses, leading to an increase in body size in order to project accurately the deeper tones of the extra lower strings. Around 1800, some odd guitar-related instruments, particularly lyre guitars (pp50-54), popularised the use of six single strings, and this seems to have spread quickly to normal guitars. This and the adoption of pin bridges, fan-strutted tops and metal frets completed the transition to a stronger, more powerful instrument, and one that a guitarist today would recognise.

NICOLAS MORLOT guitar c1820
Made in Mirecourt, France

Bambina The unusual Bambina guitar designed by Catharina Josepha Pratten (née Pelzer) was a tiny instrument. For example, the nut-to-bridge string length measures just a little over 13 inches, compared to the 25½ inches of a standard classical guitar. It was designed to be tuned an octave higher than normal.

'BAMBINA' guitar c1870
Probably made in France

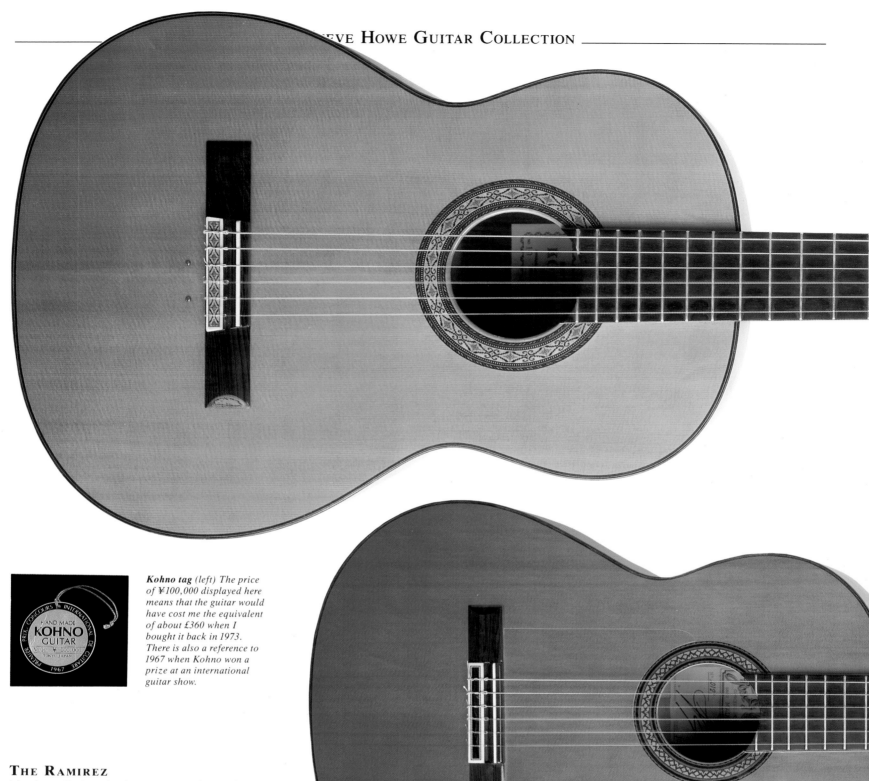

Kohno tag *(left) The price
of ¥100,000 displayed here
means that the guitar would
have cost me the equivalent
of about £360 when I
bought it back in 1973.
There is also a reference to
1967 when Kohno won a
prize at an international
guitar show.*

THE RAMIREZ

I bought my Ramirez when I was on tour in Spain with Asia,
probably in 1982, from a music shop in San Sebastian. The 1A has
been the leading Ramirez concert guitar for many years. There were
two in the shop when I visited: one was a classical and the other
this flamenco. John Wetton had come with me and was going to
have whichever of the two I didn't want. I couldn't decide, but
eventually I chose the flamenco because it provided a good contrast
to my Kohno. Flamenco guitars tend to be lightweight and have a
low action, aiding the percussive sound for which they're renowned.

Often when I first get a guitar I have a period of intense
enthusiasm for it, and I'll play it all the time – and that was
certainly the case with the Ramirez. But then I put it aside and went
back to the Kohno. So it's not quite so precious to me as the Kohno,
and although it's a very fine guitar and I would not want it to go
astray, I'm a bit more relaxed with guitars like this that are not
among what I call my premium recording guitars.

Ramirez *(above) This
Spanish family's long
history of guitar making
began in Madrid in the
latter 19th century, with
brothers José and Manuel.
Gradually production grew,
and by 1990 Ramirez, run* *by José III and José IV and
employing many extra
workers, were making over
1000 guitars per year. More
recently Ramirez have
returned once more to a
much smaller family-based
operation.*

KOHNO NO.10 1973

No. 10 produced 1969-1980

Kohno *(below) Japanese guitar-maker Masaru Kohno learned his trade in the Madrid workshop of Arcángel Fernández, and set up his own business in Tokyo around 1968. Since then he has become the leading Japanese maker of classical guitars.*

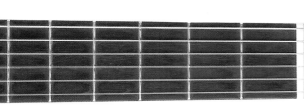

MATHEIAS lute 1977

Conde *(left) This was a one-off performance with Dave Palmer and Philamusica in an art gallery in 1972 of his 'When Wenceslas Looked Out'. I'm playing a Conde flamenco guitar, on which I also recorded 'Mood For A Day' for Yes's Fragile, but which at a later date I decided to sell.*

RAMIREZ 1A flamenco guitar 1976

Serial: 10121
1A produced c1958-current

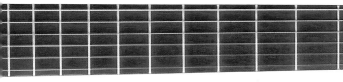

THE KOHNO

I bought the Kohno model No.10 new from a shop in Tokyo on the first Japanese Yes tour, in 1973, and it quickly became my main classical guitar. I found it to be a really pleasing guitar, and I've recorded all my work on Spanish guitar since 1973 on it.

There had been quite an important Spanish solo on the third side of *Topographic Oceans*, 'The Ancient', and I'm pretty sure I hired in a guitar on which to play that. I remember going in with a Julian Bream record and saying to our producer Eddie Offord that my guitar had to sound like that. But I've recorded all kinds of Spanish guitar parts with the Kohno since then, such as 'Surface Tension' from *The Steve Howe Album*, 'Birthright' on *ABWH*, 'Aqua Pt 1' from Asia's *Aqua* album, and 'Mood for A Day' on *Symphonic Music Of Yes*. Also, I've used the Kohno on stage a lot, including the entire first half of the concerts on my 1993 UK solo tour.

The acoustic sections of the title track on my first solo album, *Beginnings*, are mainly played on the Kohno, although in the middle

I play Coral Sitar and steel guitar. Patrick Moraz did the orchestral arrangement, and expanded the middle section, so I decided not to play the Spanish there. It was quite a task recording that piece at Morgan studios in north London. Sometimes Patrick and I asked the orchestra to 'bend' with the rhythm – the conductor would watch me and act accordingly. All the structured bits were in time, of course, but others weren't. This kind of thing tends to make an orchestra restless, and they were watching the clock for their tea-break even more avidly than usual. But it was something I really wanted to do, and a great experience.

On Yes's *Tormato*, which we recorded in 1978, I got the distinct feeling that Rick Wakeman and I were groping around for some of the time – Rick for sounds, and me for parts. Also, this was the time when I felt that the synthesiser really began to interfere with my guitar work and impinge on my territory. So I loved it when we came to work on 'Madrigal', where Rick played harpsichord and I played my Kohno, because I knew the sound was right.

Matheias *(above) The lute has always attracted me as an instrument, because it's related to the guitar, but delivers a quite different sound: a mellower tone that instantly evokes a medieval atmosphere. This one I bought in Paris in 1977, and I also have an electric lute made by a friend, Bart Nagel, which sadly we cannot show in this book as it was undergoing extensive repairs. I have used lute sparingly on record, for example on side two of Topographic Oceans, which is one of the rare occasions when the lute has made it into the mix on a Yes L.P.*

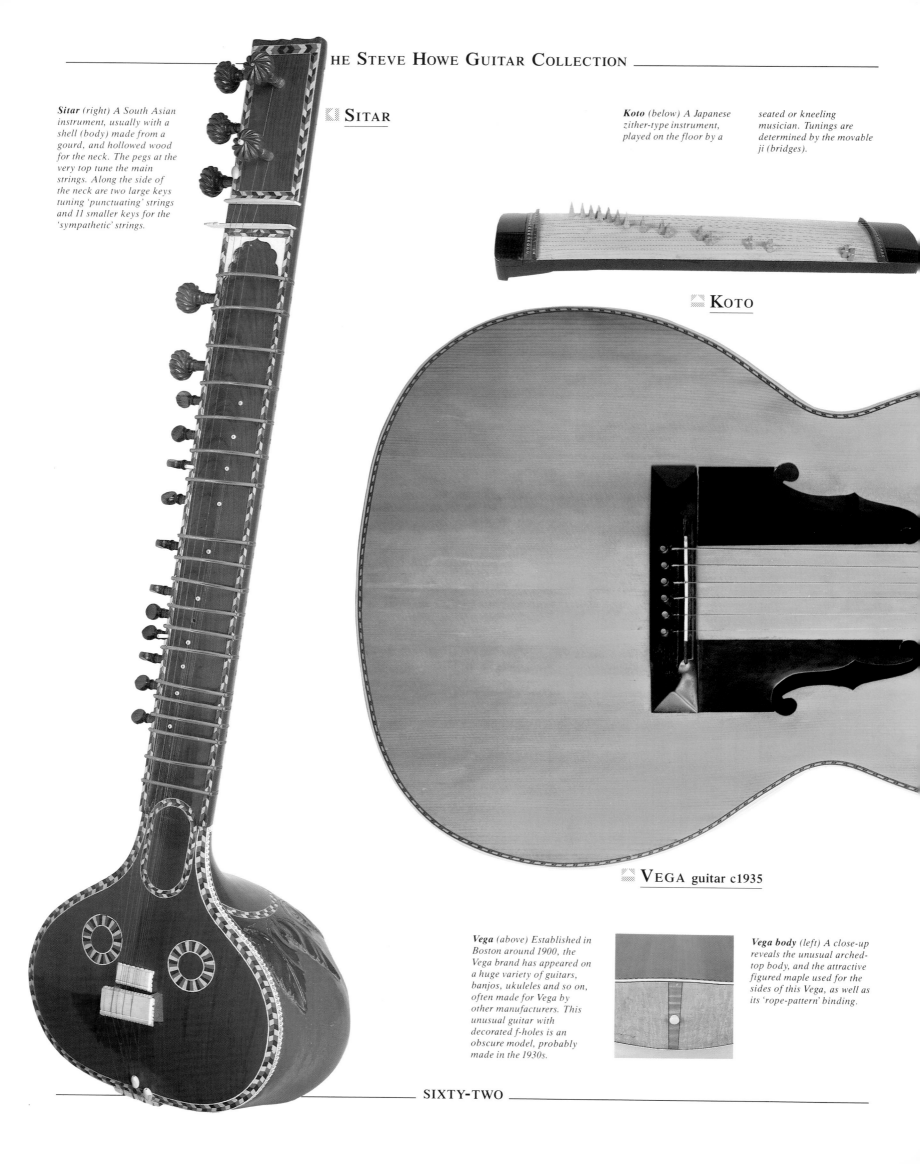

Sitar (right) A South Asian instrument, usually with a shell (body) made from a gourd, and hollowed wood for the neck. The pegs at the very top tune the main strings. Along the side of the neck are two large keys tuning 'punctuating' strings and 11 smaller keys for the 'sympathetic' strings.

▨ SITAR

Koto (below) A Japanese zither-type instrument, played on the floor by a seated or kneeling musician. Tunings are determined by the movable ji (bridges).

▨ KOTO

▨ VEGA guitar c1935

Vega (above) Established in Boston around 1900, the Vega brand has appeared on a huge variety of guitars, banjos, ukuleles and so on, often made for Vega by other manufacturers. This unusual guitar with decorated f-holes is an obscure model, probably made in the 1930s.

Vega body (left) A close-up reveals the unusual arched-top body, and the attractive figured maple used for the sides of this Vega, as well as its 'rope-pattern' binding.

12 (right) I asked for three single-coils on this custom order because I wanted a sort of '12-string Strat' sound. Steinberger's clever Trac Tuner bridge has a single large tuning knob that slides along to engage with each string in turn.

STEINBERGER 12-STRING September 1989

Serial: N8792
Custom order

Steinberger In 1982 Ned Steinberger launched a radical small-bodied headless bass model, later adding guitars. Steinberger sold to Gibson in 1987.

Six-string (below) The M Series was designed by Steinberger with Mike Rutherford of Genesis and guitar-maker Roger Giffin.

STEINBERGER GM4T September 1989

Serial: N9076
GM4T produced 1988-current

YAMAHA BB400SF fretless bass c1985

Serial: 137071
BB400SF produced 1983-1986

Yamaha (above) This century-old Japanese company first made electric guitars during the 1960s, emerging as a serious competitor to US makers in the 1970s by combining quality and originality.

I used the Steinberger six-string live with ABWH straight away, and it's quite prominent on *Grand Scheme* (the leads on 'Blinded By Science', and 'Desire Comes First' but for a little Telecaster). I used the 12 on *Turbulence*, although that's also got quite a lot of Rickenbacker 12 on it, and on *Union* it appears on 'Holding On'.

GUITAR HISTORY

Every time I heard a fretless bass on record I kept thinking that I ought to get one; I finally got the Yamaha, and I've used it on *Turbulence* and *Grand Scheme* (for example 'Luck Of The Draw').

I've had the sitar a long time, bought at the Man Ray shop in London's Covent Garden to replace the one I played on Tomorrow's 'Real Life Permanent Dream'. I got the koto in the mid 1970s, and first used it on 'Heat Of The Moment' on *Asia*.

I bought the Vega around 1977 from Peter Redding, an English guitar maker, who'd found the instrument and restored it. It sounds wonderful, and it's a piece of guitar history.

BODYWORK

I got the Steinbergers when I was on tour with ABWH in 1989. More and more people were telling me that I ought to try them, and Leslie West played one on the *Night Of The Guitars* tour I did in 1988 and I thought it sounded great. Steinberger's tiny bodiless original guitars didn't appeal to me, but the M Series had proper bodies and I liked those much more. Steinberger brought some guitars to me at a gig, and I ordered a six-string and 12-string.

They were a turning point. I seem to be able to forget that I've been playing for 30 years and running about the fingerboard, somehow it's like a new way of looking at the guitar. They're very practical: perfect intonation, beautiful sound, active EQ, loads of presence, and they work great with processors. They seemed to be the right guitars at the right time. I wasn't sure about the six-string's tremolo arm at first – it seemed very sensitive – but now I'm used to it, and to some extent it's weaned me off my Strat.

Portuguese (right) I know nothing about the maker of this 12-string instrument, as it has no label or other mark to help identify it. My sister brought it back from a holiday in Spain and gave it to me as a present when I was about 15, and really she could not have found a more useful gift if she'd tried. I used it on many of the early Yes albums and tours to great effect, without really knowing what it was. Much later I discovered that the design is typical of the indigenous Portuguese 12-string guitar.

SKD (above) The S is for Scharpach; K for maker Kasha who influenced construction; D for Django Reinhardt whose Selmer inspired the shape.

◁ ANONYMOUS Portuguese 12-string guitar c1961

On stage (right) I'm playing the Portuguese 12-string on Yes's first American tour, at an outdoor concert on the East Coast, July 1971.

JANGLING PORTUGUESE

My sister Stella came back from a holiday in Spain with the pear-shaped 12-string (left) in the early 1960s. I didn't really know what it was exactly for ages, and on *The Yes Album* I had the nerve to credit it as a 'vachalia', or vihuela, which is in fact an unusual form of the early five-course guitar – and nothing like this Portuguese 12-string at all! But that was down to limited availability in those days of information to find out what an instrument was. I didn't know where to look. But eventually I found out that it was correct to call it, simply, a Portuguese 12-string guitar, because my friend Paul Sutin has a similar one. Mine is pear shaped and small, something like a mandola size, I suppose. It was very astute of my sister to buy it, as at the time I didn't have any kind of Spanish guitar. A great present. All I've had to do to it was to replace the original thin metal bridge with something more substantial, plus it has a Barcus Berry pickup.

I've used it a lot, but the very first time I ever recorded it was on

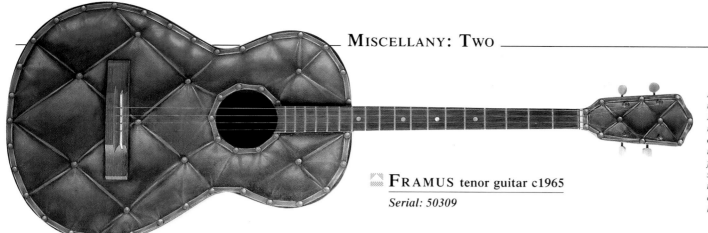

FRAMUS tenor guitar c1965
Serial: 50309

Framus (left) This German maker was established in 1946, and soon gained a reputation for acoustic and electric archtop guitars of reasonable quality. The flat-tops, like this spectacularly refinished tenor guitar, are slightly less common. Framus ceased business in the early 1980s.

Scharpach (left) Based in Bergeyk, near Eindhoven, in Holland, Theo Scharpach has been making guitars since 1977. He currently produces between 10 and 15 custom-made instruments per year, specialising in steel- and nylon-strung flat-top acoustics. Theo has also developed the Applied Acoustics system, combining a bridge piezo pickup with an internal microphone capsule, linked to external pre-amps in a rack unit.

SCHARPACH SKD July 1992
Serial: 155
SKD produced 1985-current

Levin body (left) The shape is clearly influenced by Martin's wide-waisted Dreadnought design, a generally much-copied acoustic body style.

LEVIN LTS5 12-string c1967
LTS5 produced c1965-c1975

Levin (above) Set up by Hermann Carlson Levin in Gothenburg, Sweden, the Levin company made medium priced flat-top acoustics. These were widely available in Europe, especially the UK, during the 1960s and into the 1970s when Levin was owned by Martin until closed in 1978.

'Your Move', the first part of 'I've Seen All Good People' on *The Yes Album*. It gave me a certain sort of jangly acoustic sound that I couldn't seem to get out of an ordinary 12-string. I have the Portuguese 12-string tuned in a peculiar way, which I came to by trial and error. The top string's tuned to A-flat, above the guitar, and then it goes E, B, E, B, E. The first three pairs are tuned in unison – two A-flats, two Es, two Bs – then the next E is split high and low, B high and low, and the E is the same pitch as the fourth course, split high and low. So it's really without a bass end, and ends up with this lovely rich jangly sound.

The Portuguese 12-string is also on 'And You And I' from *Close To The Edge*, a track where Yes explored its acoustic side rather well, I think. There's some colouring from it on the first side of *Topographic Oceans*, and 'Wonderous Stories' on *Going For The One* is based around a rhythm part on that guitar.

I'm pretty sure that I bought the Levin 12-string in the late 1960s, and it's possible that I may have played it on some of my earlier records, like Tomorrow. My memory is a bit hazy on how I actually came upon it. But it fell into disrepair, and maybe that's why when we came to record 'And You And I' for *Close To The Edge* I borrowed Chris Squire's Guild, and didn't use the Levin. The Levin was in a bit of a state, so I had Sam Li do it up around 1975, and it's now in fantastic condition. I almost didn't recognise it when it came back. I've never used the Levin in performance, but it has been to various sessions so it may well be the jingle-jangle in the background of some tracks. I certainly used it at the end of 'Turn Of The Century' on *Going For The One* for a very jangly acoustic 12-string sound amid Rick Wakeman's pleasant electric piano chords. *Going For The One* really is one of my favourite Yes albums.

THE SCHARPACH SKD

I produced guitarist Martin Taylor's *Artistry* album in 1992, and he told me about Theo Scharpach, an excellent Dutch guitar maker. So I arranged to see Theo, and he came to my hotel with two guitars, one of which was very similar to the one I have now, the SKD model. I sat down with it... and everything around me sort of stopped! Wow! It played like a beauty, the cutaway is fantastic with no restrictions in your access to the top end. It has an exceptional sound with wonderful dynamics: it has a delicate side, but is able to be powerful too. Actually, I play my Scharpach rather more gently than I normally play, and with slightly lighter strings.

So I raved about this Scharpach guitar and said to Theo, yes, I'd like you to build me one. I collected my guitar in November 1992, at the end of Asia's European tour for *Aqua*. I used the Scharpach all over my *Grand Scheme* album, on 'Roundabout' and 'Wonderous Stories' on *Symphonic Music Of Yes*, and on my 1993 UK solo tour.

In the mid 1970s I became interested in meeting artists, including John Ronayne who specialised in trompe l'oeil. It seemed like a good idea to try this on a guitar, so I let him loose on my Framus tenor guitar which was turned into a very unusual looking instrument, refinished by John to look like a Chesterfield.

Vox (below) The British Vox brand, better known on a series of good amplifiers, first appeared on guitars from 1960 to 1970, made in England and then Italy and Japan. The stylish Phantom and peardrop-shaped Mk VI models later became popular 'retro' guitars, but this heavily modified bass probably started life as a cheap Bassmaster model.

Guyatone *(above) This Japanese brand was established in 1933 by Mitsuo Matsuki, a fan of Hawaiian music, to make steel guitars. His nickname Guya-san, from 'douguya', meaning one who takes great care of tools, provided the company's name. The Tokyo-based firm continued business after 1946, and was among the first Japanese makers of solid electric guitars. The model shown was exported with various brands, including Guyatone, Antoria and Star.*

Syndicats *(above) My first group, which I joined in 1963. I'm playing the original Guyatone (left).*

TOMORROW, AMERICA

I got the Vox around 1967, my first bass, and Junior Wood, the bass player in Tomorrow, adopted it for the LP. The first song I ever played bass on was 'The Kid Was A Killer', a B-side for Keith West (released July 1968), playing the Vox. But I mainly used it for bass parts in my own musical constructions. I got a Revox tape recorder in 1970 that I still have, and I used to dub from track to track and write songs and instrumentals in that way.

Hayman gave me the 2020 which I used for Yes's recording of Paul Simon's 'America' for *The New Age Of Atlantic*. That's one of the few places to hear the full-length version: the end of the guitar break is on my 175, but the first two-thirds or more is the Hayman. It was an opportunity to play an American-style solo with more of the clichés I'd been so busily leaving out. There are things in it from Duane Eddy to Delaney & Bonnie, re-interpreted. I used the Hayman because, somehow, changing guitars quite often freed me from a possible over-association with the 175.

Vox body (above) I bought this in the late 1960s, my first bass, and it became my experimental guitar. I added a couple of pickups, I think a Rickenbacker and a Hayman, and had Sam Li take it down to its natural and rather ghastly wood finish.

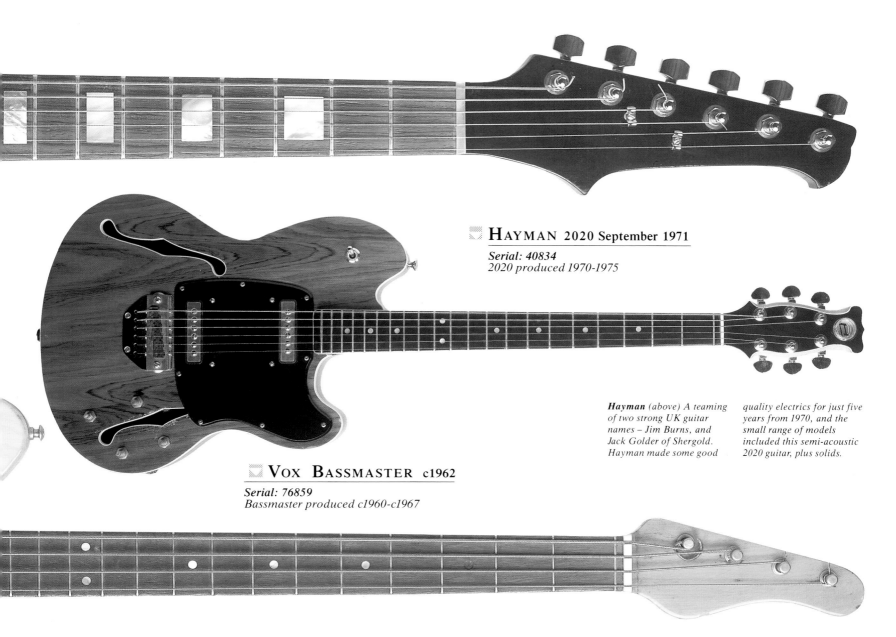

GUYATONE LG50 c1960
LG50 produced c1958-c1963

HAYMAN 2020 September 1971
Serial: 40834
2020 produced 1970-1975

Hayman (above) A teaming of two strong UK guitar names – Jim Burns, and Jack Golder of Shergold. Hayman made some good quality electrics for just five years from 1970, and the small range of models included this semi-acoustic 2020 guitar, plus solids.

VOX BASSMASTER c1962
Serial: 76859
Bassmaster produced c1960-c1967

THE TWO GUYATONES

When I was 12 my parents bought me my very first guitar, a little f-hole acoustic of unknown make. But I was hearing Link Wray, Chet Atkins was beginning to come on the scene, and a lot of those sounds you just couldn't make on an acoustic. I needed an electric guitar. So around 1961, after about two years of playing the acoustic, I got my first electric, a Guyatone. Not the one I own now, but very similar. I remember the sheer excitement of getting an electric guitar, and a matching amp with tremolo. I bought the two from a friend of mine, Sean Manchester, for around £15.

I played the original Guyatone in my first group, The Syndicats, and I also had a Burns Jazz electric about that time. We used to play around north London, at a pub called The Swan in Tottenham, and a club at Pentonville Prison every week, from early 1963. Our efforts in blues got more intense, and we dropped our R&B stuff and got into Jimmy Reed and John Lee Hooker. We made some singles with producer Joe Meek, when I was 17. I played Guyatone on

'Maybellene' (March 1964) but by 'Howlin For My Baby' (January 1965) I was using my new Gibson ES175D (see p8). That was the period when I would use the 175 and sometimes swap to the Guyatone for a different sound.

Then I had the frets of that Guyatone filed down to try to make it play better, but I thought the guy ruined it and I quickly traded it for a Gibson Melody Maker. Around 1967 I bought another Guyatone, the one I still own. I used it with Tomorrow, and soon plastered it with psychedelic paint and pictures. That guitar hung around for quite a while. Then Sam Li worked on the guitar for me. He made it shiny black and put on a black scratchplate, and I'd sawn off part of the headstock, so he repaired that too.

My Guyatone has a wonderful sound, and I used it on 'Perpetual Change', on *The Yes Album*. The guitar was on call for a more Fender-like, wiry sound, which you can hear on that track. The group get frantically out of control as does the guitar, freaking out in an Indian sitar style as the track fades to another section.

Studio (above) Here I am trying out the Vox bass as I listen to a track in my headphones during one of the sessions for The Steve Howe Album at Morgan Studios in north London, in 1979.

Body (left) The 13 extra strings are tuned semitones apart. They're designed to resonate sympathetically and help to emulate a real sitar sound.

Guitar tree Michael Tait (below) was Yes's inventor, light and stage designer, master of all things. Whatever Yes needed, he would make. So he put together my guitar 'tree' for the Topographic tour. Before that I had the Coral Sitar on a separate stand and the Fender steel on legs, but now I needed my Danelectro 12-string too. So we came up with the circular tree, a very good one-tour solution. It had the Sitar, 12-string and steel fixed to three 'arms'. I could push them out of my way when I was playing the Junior (right), or pull around one of the three into a playing position.

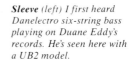

Sleeve (left) I first heard Danelectro six-string bass playing on Duane Eddy's records. He's seen here with a UB2 model.

◥ DANELECTRO 3612S SHORT HORN six-string bass c1965

Short Horn six-string bass produced c1963-1967

Short Horn (above) The company's single-cutaway UB2 model of 1956 introduced the six-string bass, effectively a guitar tuned an octave lower than normal. This 'Short Horn' double-cutaway version was a later addition to the Danelectro line.

CORAL SITAR c1968

Serial: 825066
Sitar produced 1967-1970

Sitar (above) Designed with guitarist Vinnie Bell's patented 'flat' bridge that gives a buzzy sitar sound.

Live (above) I'm playing the Coral Sitar on the tree, late in 1973. You can see the tree 'arm' fixed to it. I've got two Sitars: the one pictured above had work done to the body in order to fit it to the tree; the mint example pictured left I bought later as a backup.

DANELECTRO DANE/HAWK A2N12 c1967

Dane/Hawk A2N12 produced c1966-1968

12-string (left) Variously described as a Hawk or Dane model, this Danelectro has pickup covers apparently made from re-cycled lipstick tubes. A damaged area from the mounting for the guitar tree can be seen on the lower body.

Danelectro New Yorker Nathan I Daniel produced his first Danelectro guitars around 1955, also building instruments under brands such as Silvertone for mail-order companies. Daniel's guitars were often boldly styled and, while cheap, using basic materials such as masonite (hardboard), they worked surprisingly well. Daniel sold out to MCA in 1967. MCA applied their record label name Coral to some guitars, including the electric Sitar designed by guitarist Vinnie Bell (real name Vincent Gambella). MCA then sold Danelectro to one Magnus Hendell, who pulled the plug in 1970, the year of the last Danelectro.

SIX AND TWELVE

I first played a Danelectro six-string bass in the early 1960s when I used to spend time in Selmer's music shop in central London. One of the guys heard me and asked if I'd like to demonstrate it. I remember playing it deafeningly loud through an enormous Selmer amp set-up... and people would come in off the street to see what was going on. I had such confidence then, but I don't think I was even aware of it.

I may have had my Danelectro six-string bass since the 1960s, but I first used it on record on 'Break Away From It All' on *Beginnings*, and to double guitar on various other tracks since.

I bought the Danelectro 12-string at a shop called The Guitar Center in Los Angeles while on tour with Yes, probably in 1972. I plugged the guitar in and it sounded unbelievably good. I bought it, took it back to our hotel – the Hyatt, the musicians' hotel, known then as the Riot – and I played it through a Gibsonette amp that I bought at the same time. It sounded remarkable.

For me, electric 12-string had started with The Byrds, and nobody really made the Rickenbacker sound better. Then I heard the Danelectro and wondered if this was how it should have sounded – and anyway, I didn't have a Rickenbacker at the time, the Dano was my first electric 12-string. I used it as the main electric guitar on side two of *Topographic Oceans*.

Later I use it tuned to open-E to play the solo in 'Sketches In The Sun' on *GTR*. Unfortunately that album is digitally recorded, which in theory should make it sound better, but with certain sounds and certain inadequate digital knowledge, it can sound horrible. So it's not a very satisfactory sound on that track, although when I was standing in the studio it was exactly the sound I wanted. The Danelectro 12 also sounds good when you hear it on the video of *Night Of The Guitars*. I played it straight into the desk, and you can hear that there's a good body to the sound. But on reflection, the Danelectro was a stop-gap before I got my other 12-strings, the Rickenbacker (p84) and later the Steinberger (p62).

ELECTRIC SITAR

I got my original Coral Sitar on a Yes tour of America, probably in 1972. I'd heard electric sitar on some records in the 1960s, such as 'Green Tambourine' by The Lemon Pipers, and really liked the sound. The Coral has a special bridge to give the 'sitar' sound. It makes tuning and intonation just about impossible, but you can make it work if you persevere. It produces a basic, exotic sound.

I bought another later in the 1970s as I thought the first one might give up on me, especially after Mickey Tait and I sawed into it in an aborted effort to make a twin-neck with the Danelectro 12-string. I walked into Manny's in New York and they had an as-new Coral for just $200. I could hardly avoid walking out with it.

The electric Sitar first turned up on record on 'Siberian Khatru' (*Close To The Edge*). I used to record things on my own at home in north London with my Revox tape recorder, and a solo from one of the things I recorded became part of my contribution to 'Siberian Khatru'. As far as I recall that track was one of the first things we recorded for the album. Sometimes the studio is the place where everything happens, and that's usually the case with electric sitar. You can't make it sound any good through an amp, in my experience, you've got to plug it direct into the recording board.

I also used the Coral Sitar to get the structure going on 'Break Away From It All' on *Beginnings*, and in a later section of that piece there's a lot of tracked-up sitars, and they really build the tension. More recently I used Coral on *The Grand Scheme* album, for the main riffs on 'Blinded By Science', and quite predominantly on 'Too Much Is Taken And Not Enough Given'.

G-brand (above) The earliest 6120 models came complete with a 'branded' G for Gretsch, echoing the wild-west theme of a guitar aimed at country pickers.

Sleeve (left) Proof that the home studio is not a recent phenomenon, this 1950s LP has a moody Chet Atkins hugging his Gretsch 6120 amid the recording technology of the time. Note also the socks.

Gretsch ad (left) Chet Atkins lent his name not only to the hollow-body 6120, but also to the semi- solid 6121. This wild-west version of Gretsch's Jet guitars was launched in 1954, a year before this ad.

CHET ATKINS & NEIL YOUNG

I first got into Gretsch through hearing Chet Atkins, when I was about 14, and his clear picking sound was the best I'd heard. But I didn't rush out and buy a Gretsch. I must have known that I wouldn't sound like Chet just by buying a Gretsch, that it wasn't quite that simple. Come the 1970s, when I started buying the guitars that I wanted, I got this lovely 6120 for $400 from George Gruhn's shop in Nashville, Tennessee.

I first used the 6120 on 'Break Away From It All' on Beginnings, in the main guitar break section, and with those mournful bends in the solo I suppose my reference there was Neil Young, my other favourite Gretsch player. If you play as if you don't have a clear mind – which is generally how I like to sound, as if I'm just going forward through the notes – then Neil Young might well come into view. I had the pleasure of meeting Neil Young at the Philadelphia Spectrum about ten years ago, a very interesting guy. I respect him because he's still not necessarily adhering to the rules.

I've used the 6120 on various other projects: it's on 'Jekyll & Hyde' from GTR, and I took it on the GTR tour in 1986. I got a bit cheeky In New York, and instead of doing my 'Clap' solo spot on the Martin, out came the 6120. I talked about Chet Atkins and started playing a selection of Chet-style pieces, and really got a buzz out of it. But the lack of familiarity I still have for a Gretsch fingerboard means that after a couple of nights it was giving me hell, and I stopped. The 6120 has made a handful of other appearances, including 'Fine Line' from Turbulence, and 'The Fall Of Civilisation' (main riff) from The Grand Scheme.

I got the Super Chet new from Manny's store in New York, because it was a really attractive guitar. It's almost as good as the 6120, and in fact sometimes I find I'm more at home on it, although the 6120 sounds more exacting and what you expect a Gretsch to be. I've always found Gretsch fingerboards too flat, and I've often wondered about the possibility of having a Gretsch with a Gibson neck. Why not? We could call it a Gibetsch.

GRETSCH 6120 CHET ATKINS 1955

Serial: missing
6120 Hollow Body produced 1971-1980

Gretsch *(below) German immigrant Friedrich Gretsch set up his company in New York in 1883, the first guitars appearing in* the 1920s. Gretsch's best known electrics were launched in the 1950s, like this Chet Atkins-endorsed 6120, launched in 1954.

Sleeve *(above) Teensville is the most important guitar album I ever bought. For me Chet was the originator,* and this 1960 record started me off. It made me realise you can do anything on a guitar, that the sky's the limit.

GRETSCH 7691 SUPER CHET 1974

Serial: 9.4031
Super Chet produced 1971-1980

Super Chet *(above) This deluxe model was the result of a collaboration between the new Gretsch owners, Baldwin, and Chet Atkins.*

Model 7691 *(above) In 1967 Gretsch were taken over by the Baldwin company, who continued to make Gretsches until 1981. Guitars made before Baldwin stepped in have 6000-series model numbers (the 6120, above left, for example), while Baldwin-era Gretsches are in the 7000 range, like this 7691 Super Chet. Several sporadic and unsuccessful attempts were made to re-launch Gretsch guitars after 1981, but following the buy-back of the company by the Gretsch family in 1985, Japanese production of a re-organised Gretsch range began during 1990.*

GRETSCH 6025 BIKINI twin-neck 1961

Serial: 40815
Bikini twin-neck produced 1961-1962

Bikini *(above) The bizarre Bikinis came in single or double-neck versions, with a folding 'butterfly' body back and interchangeable slot-in bass and guitar necks. "Complete flexibility* with guitar and bass in a single portable unit!" read the publicity. I bought this because it was rare and unusual, but quickly sold it on when I realised it was of little practical use.

00-18 (below) Switzerland, 1976, with my son Dylan, who would have been seven, peeping through the window. The damage to the 00-18's body is visible, but

Martin did some excellent repair work on it about six years later. They replaced a section of wood on the body, bringing it to the fine state that you see above.

Martin (above) Christian Frederick Martin was born in Germany in 1796, and worked for various luthiers before emigrating to the United States in 1833, setting up a music shop in New York. He soon moved to Nazareth, Pennsylvania, where Martin's factory remains today.

On tour (left) A snapshot taken in an anonymous hotel room during Yes's debut American tour in summer 1971, and my first ever visit to the United States. I'm strumming the 00-18, which I'd had for about three years at this point. I used it on the tour for my solo spot.

A NEW ACOUSTIC VOICE

In 1968 I played a good Martin for the first time, and I had no doubt at all that I'd met the acoustic guitar I'd been searching for. Until then I'd only played f-hole archtop acoustics, plus a few dreadful 'folk' flat-tops. But the influence that steered me in the right direction was Paul Simon. I would listen to the beautiful guitar sound on Simon & Garfunkel's *Bookends* album, and I found out that Paul Simon used a Martin.

Martin was a very traditional company then, and had hardly changed since the mid 1930s or so. I wasn't up to date with them: Martin catalogues were not easily available in England, and while I'd seen one or two guitars in shops, they seemed to be very scarce instruments. Also, some Martins are very plain guitars, and I think that put me off them at first. I thought I'd have a more grand looking acoustic. Eventually, of course, that very plainness appealed to me, and in a way the 00-18 model seems to me to be Martin's Telecaster: a very *working* guitar.

BUYING THE 00-18

In summer 1968 I saw an ad in the *Melody Maker* for a Martin 00-18 for £125, in a shop called Take Five, opposite Sound City in Shaftesbury Avenue, central London. I went along, played it... and that was that. I rushed home with it on the train, and I was absolutely elated to have this wonderful guitar. The 175 didn't come off its pedestal, that was untouchable, but this was the acoustic sound I wanted. From then on I saw my Gibson 175 and Martin 00-18 as my two key guitars. With the Martin I'd found the acoustic voice I wanted, a really important sound. I think the Martin sound is perfect, and I still do.

I went on a very, very long run with my Martin 00-18, and I played it constantly in studios and on stages for very nearly 25 years. Lately I've been resting the guitar, mainly because the bridge is worn out and it needs to go back to Martin again for more work and another general overhaul. I'm pleased to have found a great new flat-top acoustic guitar in the Scharpach (see p64).

MARTIN 00-18 September 1953

Serial: 132552
00-18 produced c1877-current

00-18 (below) *Martin's model codes usually have a prefix indicating the body size, plus a number indicating the Martin 'style'. Generally, the higher* *the style number, the fancier the finishing. Thus 00 indicates a medium sized Martin body, and 18 denotes a relatively plain finish.*

Ad (left) *Part of a page from the back of the Melody Maker dated 14th September 1968. This is where I spotted my 00-18 for sale at Take Five, a shop in an area of central London well known for music stores.*

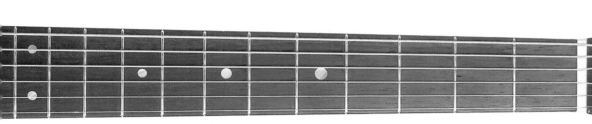

MARTIN 00-18T tenor guitar November 1947

Serial: 102972
00-18T produced 1931-1948

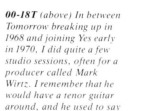

00-18T (above) *In between Tomorrow breaking up in 1968 and joining Yes early in 1970, I did quite a few studio sessions, often for a producer called Mark Wirtz. I remember that he would have a tenor guitar around, and he used to say there was always a musical* *place for it. It's fun to have a tenor, but in fact I've rarely used mine. Tenor guitars had only four strings and a short scale-length, and as the name implies were pitched lower than normal. They're rarely seen today, and Martin's are probably the best.*

On stage (above) With the 00-18, probably late 1970s, in the midst of 'Clap' during my regular concert solo spot.

USING THE 00-18

As one of my key guitars, the 00-18 has been used on many recordings and tours, and I'd like to highlight one or two here. Within a year of getting the Martin I wrote 'Clap' on it, which I still think is the best composition I'll write in my life – and if that does turn out to be the case, I won't be disappointed. On *The Yes Album* we used a live recording of 'Clap' made at a concert at the Lyceum in London. It seemed novel to have a live track on the record, and in fact I don't recall recording a studio version. It's also 00-18 for the acoustic guitar part on 'Yours Is No Disgrace' (*The Yes Album*) and on 'Roundabout' (*Fragile*).

On 'Awaken' from *Going For The One* you can hear me playing double-tracked 00-18 with an E-Bow, a hand-held unit that gave infinite sustain on single notes, and I make some very odd backwards-type sounds. I'd like to think that's my forte: not just playing notes on the guitar, but having fun with them too.

'Turn Of The Century' on *Going For The One* was a mammoth construction and very complicated to record. One day we improvised across the number, and out of that I wrote and re-recorded a guitar part that seemed to work with the singing. The 00-18 really came through for that, and I think it's one of the Martin's best recordings ever. It was the first album without Eddie Offord producing; we had John Timperley as main engineer, plus Dave Richards who's since recorded David Bowie, Queen and many others.

I'd noticed on the Yes *Union* tour of 1991 ('around the world in 80 dates') how everyone kept playing the same thing every night in their solo spot. I think when you play on your own that one of the great advantages is being able to change things – which I did. So when we got to Milan I played Vivaldi on the 00-18, 'Winter' from *The Four Seasons* – and when the audience caught on they flipped out! Then in Japan I played a different piece every night, some obscure, some album tracks, some songs, all sorts of things. It's great to put yourself to the test like that, and I really got a buzz out of it. And in a way that's what it's all about.

SOM-45 (above) A re-issue of Martin's early OM design, their first with a 14th-fret neck/body join, giving better high-fret access. This SOM is in Style 45, one of Martin's most decorative, liberally adorned with exquisite abalone inlay.

SOM-45 (above) A re-issue of the 1929-1934 OM 'Orchestra Model'. The original idea came from a banjo player who asked for a Martin that was audible in orchestras, and had more accessible frets and a narrower neck to which banjo players could adapt.

MARTIN 000-45 March 1927

Serial: 30359
000-45 produced c1905-1942, 1971-1985

MARTIN J12-65M 1985

Serial: 456261
J12-65M produced 1985-current

2-27 (above) Today we're more familiar with the body sizes that Martin calls 0, 00, 000 and D, but this very early size 2 guitar is an example of one of the smallest bodies that Martin produced. The trend toward larger guitars meant that few size 2 Martins were made after the 1930s.

Coupa (below) This was also featured in the Tom Evans book 'Guitars' and described as having a combination of features unique on a Martin.

Coupa (above) It was around 1970 that my brother-in-law, Les Payne, found this guitar for sale, and after John Bailey did some restoration work I bought it. John Coupa was a guitar teacher in New York who went into business with Martin in the 1840s, probably acting as a sales agent. This seems to be a transitional or experimental Martin instrument: features such as the headstock are typical of their 1840s style, while the body shape is rarely seen until later, and constructional details have a strong Spanish influence. It's a very important historical piece.

MARTIN & COUPA c1845

Ukulele (right) The ukulele craze peaked in the States in the 1920s, and during that time Martin often made more ukes than guitars. I had an idea that this ukulele might provide an extra texture on recordings, but it's never quite made the mix. I suppose what I really wanted was a very decorative Martin uke, and this seemed like a sort of half-way house.

■ **MARTIN STYLE** 3 ukulele c197

Style 3 ukulele produced 1916-current

MARTIN MC-28 1982

Serial: 438593
MC-28 produced 1981-current

Ad (left) A clever idea from an early 1980s publicity campaign where Martin presented me with guitarist David Becker, who represented a lesser-known artist – but both relying on Martin for our acoustic guitar sound.

MC-28 (above) Martin's M series appeared in 1977, after a brief fad for converting obscure old Martin archtop guitars into flat-tops. Martin dug out the dusty archtop templates to make their new M series flat-tops. The result was a

Gibson-like jumbo outline but with a thinner body, giving power and bite but little of the bass-heaviness that a number of players dislike about Martin's big 'Dreadnought' guitars. Some M guitars have a cutaway, hence 'MC'.

MARTIN SOM-45 1977

Serial: 399031
SOM-45 produced 1977-current

Live (left) Here I'm playing my Martin J12-65M 12-string, on stage with ABWH during our American tour in the early part of 1990.

More Martins The J12-65M 12-string (above) was part of Martin's Jumbo M series, which was introduced in 1985 and, although similar to the 'waisted Dreadnought' M series (see MC-28 at top of page), had the bonus of a normal full-depth body. This gives a wonderfully rounded and balanced sound that's

especially suited to the richness of a 12-string. The 000-45 (below) is a lovely old guitar from the late 1920s. It clearly shows the original style of joining the neck to the body at the 12th fret. This has now been superseded by the 14th-fret join, which necessitates a rather wider and somewhat shorter body shape.

CUTAWAYS & TWELVES

I bought the SOM-45 in 1977 in Chicago at a shop called Wooden Music. It's a very fine guitar – no electronics, just a straight acoustic – with a tremendous brightness and brilliance. I used it in summer 1979 for the whole of a solo set I played at the Montreux Jazz Festival. I included 'Mood For A Day', 'Clap', 'Meadow Rag', 'Cactus Boogie', 'Diary Of A Man Who Disappeared', all the pieces I'd done either on solo albums or which had been merged into Yes, plus I did a cover of Big Bill Broonzy's 'The Glory Of Love'. There's a video out in Japan of the show.

I often dealt with a guy called John Marshall at Martin, and I went to see him in 1982 to look at some guitars, one of which was the MC-28 – and I just went mad on it. At last we had a cutaway Martin that had a great sound. It's not been too predominant in the studio, although I did use it on 'Sharp On Attack', an aborted GTR piece that I re-recorded for the *Guitar Speak* album. Also, I remember using MC-28 on 'Beautiful Ideas' (*Grand Scheme*) as the

guide guitar, a track you put down first and which usually gets wiped. But towards the end there's a very fast riff that I never managed to play as well again, so I left the MC-28.

I got the 000-45 in the 1970s from George Gruhn, and I remember taking it straight on holiday with me to somewhere very hot. I sat around playing it thinking, "This is it, this is it!" However, I encountered the problems that can occur when you play old guitars, that sometimes you can't get them to feel as you want them to. New strings help, obviously. I tried to get it onto records, and in the GTR days it was a prize guitar to take to the studio to see if people liked it, but it never made a noticeable impression.

It was a relief when the 12-string came along because my Guild wasn't right. I got on the phone to Martin, said I had to have a 12-string, and they sent me the J12-65M immediately. From the late 1980s that's the 12-string I've used. I played it on 'Masquerade' from *Union*, all the acoustic 12-string work on *Turbulence* and *Grand Scheme*, and on 'Wonderous Stories' from *Symphonic Music Of Yes*.

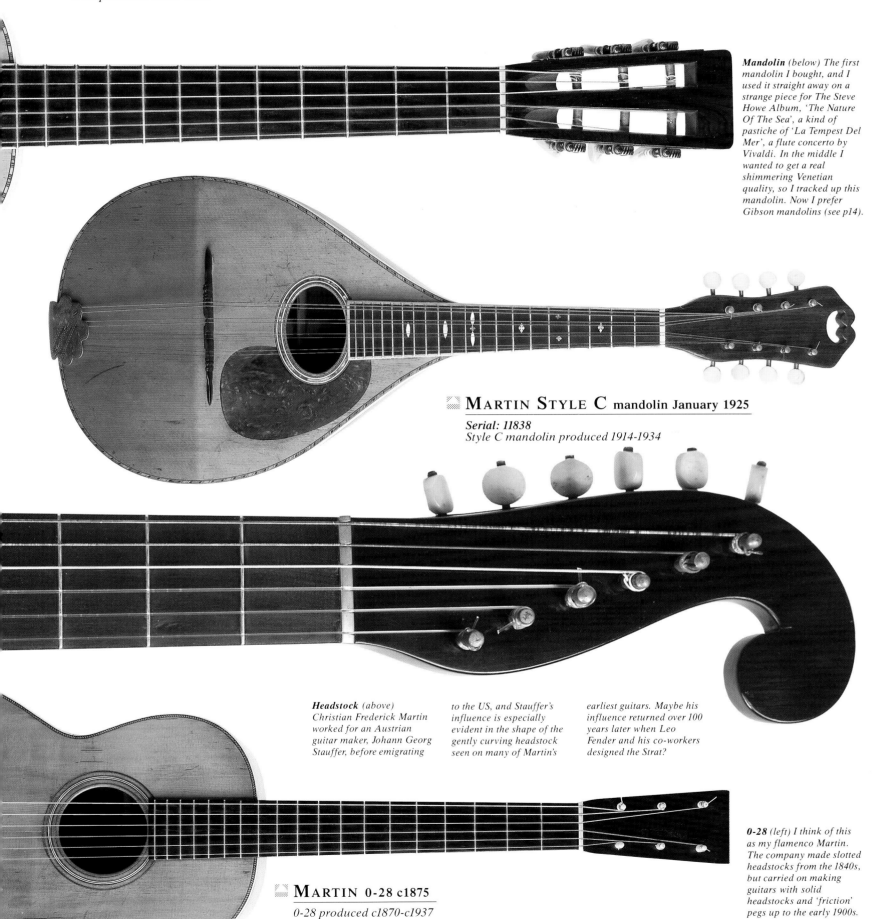

MARTIN 2-27 c1860
2-27 produced c1857-c1907

Mandolin *(below) The first mandolin I bought, and I used it straight away on a strange piece for The Steve Howe Album, 'The Nature Of The Sea', a kind of pastiche of 'La Tempest Del Mer', a flute concerto by Vivaldi. In the middle I wanted to get a real shimmering Venetian quality, so I tracked up this mandolin. Now I prefer Gibson mandolins (see p14).*

MARTIN STYLE C mandolin January 1925
Serial: 11838
Style C mandolin produced 1914-1934

Headstock *(above) Christian Frederick Martin worked for an Austrian guitar maker, Johann Georg Stauffer, before emigrating* *to the US, and Stauffer's influence is especially evident in the shape of the gently curving headstock seen on many of Martin's* *earliest guitars. Maybe his influence returned over 100 years later when Leo Fender and his co-workers designed the Strat?*

MARTIN 0-28 c1875
0-28 produced c1870-c1937

0-28 *(left) I think of this as my flamenco Martin. The company made slotted headstocks from the 1840s, but carried on making guitars with solid headstocks and 'friction' pegs up to the early 1900s.*

F212CR-NT (below) Not the most romantic name, but the suffix of this custom ordered Guild means cutaway (C), rosewood back and sides (R) and natural (NT) finish.

Guild *Alfred Dronge set up the Guild company in New York in 1952, and soon gained a good reputation for archtop electric guitars. After an influx of workers from Epiphone and a move to New Jersey in 1956, Guild also became known for fine flat-top acoustics.*

Body (above) Once again I was drawn to a guitar with a sharp 'Florentine' cutaway, recalling the general outline of my Gibson 175.

Live (right) On-stage with the Guild 12-string, probably in the late 1970s. I've just moved from the 12-string to Fender steel during 'And You And I'.

AND YOU AND I AND GUILD

I used Chris Squire's nice Guild non-cutaway 12-string to record 'And You And I'. I was cautious about getting a Guild for myself, but it worked well on the record so I decided to get one for live work. I ordered the top Guild 12-string, but with a cutaway which was a necessity for me. Guild came back and said they didn't make that particular combination at the time, but they would make me a special custom-built guitar. They put together a guitar with their fancy-inlaid F512 neck and a cutaway F212 body.

The Guild's on the solo-rendition section of 'Without You' on *Asia*, which is a nice piece that I'm rather fond of. I thought the guitar was the bee's knees for quite a while, but I tried and tried to get it amplified better, and it became difficult to use live. Also, it's a bit on the large size for me, and the spacing on the strings isn't very close, so it demanded quite a lot of effort. It gave some trouble on the earliest shows of the ABWH tour, so that's when I arranged to get my Martin 12-string (see p75) which soon took

over the role of my main acoustic 12-string.

The first use I made of the Guild D40, which I think I bought new from Manny's in New York, was on the early takes of 'Turn Of The Century' for the *Going For The One* sessions, but that part of the recording was eventually replaced by my Martin 00-18. The Guild D40 was one of a range of guitars that I often use just to get things going. It's of the wide-waisted 'Dreadnought' shape, which tends to give a guitar a rather dense, bassy tone that I've never found too attractive. So I began my experiments with Nashville tuning, which gives a full, bright sound (see also Broadcaster p42).

The name for the tuning comes from its popularity among Nashville session players who first used it to add sparkle to country guitar tracks. Essentially, it's as if you were to take away a string from each pair in a 12-string set, leaving the higher string in the case of the octave pairs. The Nashville-tuned Guild first shows up on some of the recordings on *GTR*, and it regularly comes out now on session work if I need an acoustic in a high tuning.

GUILD F212CR-NT March 1979

Serial: 203021
Custom order

12-string (below) A long headstock provides space for the six-a-side tuner arrangement, along with Guild's typical 'G' logo.

THE BANJO BEAT

I liked those early novelty banjo records from the 1930s and 1940s which would have an organ on one side and a banjo on the other. They rather inspired me to think about getting a banjo and learning to play. I found the Wilkes in a secondhand shop in north London in the 1970s, and it's the nicer of two banjos that I've had – the other one was a seven-string, but it's since disappeared. The Wilkes is a very attractive instrument to have, considering how little banjo I've ended up playing.

The Bacon & Day banjo guitar is more practical for me, because it sounds like a banjo but plays like a guitar. I got it in the 1970s too, probably in the States, although I can't remember where exactly. I first used it in the studio for my *Steve Howe Album*, on 'Alls A Chord', 'Ram' and 'Cactus Boogie'. 'Alls A Chord' had hung over from the *Beginnings* sessions, so I'd kept adding and adding bits over the years, ending up with a strange piece where the instrumentation changes every few bars. So it moves from sitar guitars to banjo guitars to Spanish guitars to electric guitars to wah-wah guitars... quite an amazing procession, really. But generally, playing the banjo has never been a big focus for me.

BACON & DAY BLUE BELL banjo guitar c1920s

F C WILKES banjo

Serial: 554967

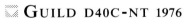

Banjos Bacon & Day (six-string banjo guitar above) was started in 1922 by banjoist Frederick Bacon and businessman David Day, and lasted until around 1940 when Gretsch bought out Bacon. Unfortunately, information is scarce about Wilkes, whose four-string banjo is pictured above.

GUILD D40C-NT 1976

Serial: 138764
D40C-NT produced 1976-1986

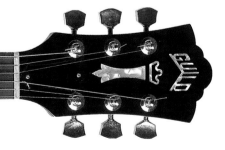

D40C-NT (above) Guild's most popular flat-tops have been this D-style, referring to the Martin Dreadnought shape, and the more traditional waisted 'jumbo' F-style (for example, the 12-string at the top of the page). Despite producing some good instruments, Guild's flat-tops have always been in the shadow of Martin and Gibson, and have never really appealed to collectors. The benefit of this is that in theory one should be able to pick up some secondhand bargains.

Roberts Custom (above) Howard Roberts (1929-1992) was a Hollywood jazz session-man who also had some success with his own groups. He helped Epiphone design this unusual guitar which uniquely combines a cutaway archtop body with an oval soundhole and a humbucking pickup. It never gained wide popularity, but a Gibson-branded version appeared in the 1970s after Epiphone ceased US production.

EPIPHONE CAIOLA c1964

Serial: 174883
Caiola produced 1963-1970

Caiola Custom (above) A model designed in collaboration with Al Caiola, a studio guitarist destined to be remembered as the man who played on the theme from Bonanza, the TV Western series. The Caiola model uses the Tonexpressor five-way tone circuit of the Professional, along with conventional volume, tone and pickup-selector. A second version, the Caiola Standard, had P90 pickups.

Broadway (below) Among the first Epiphone 'Masterbilt' models, this is the early small-body variety; the body was enlarged after about 1937. More recently, this example has had a block-inlaid fingerboard and new tuners fitted.

EPIPHONE BROADWAY c1933

Serial: 6983
Broadway produced 1931-1958

EPIPHONE HOWARD ROBERTS CUSTOM c1967

Serial: 5?1659
Howard Roberts model produced 1964-1970

Epiphone *Epaminondas Stathopoulo, a guitar maker of Greek extraction, set up Epiphone in New York around 1910, making* *guitars from the 1920s. Gibson bought the company in 1957 and made Epiphones at their Kalamazoo factory.*

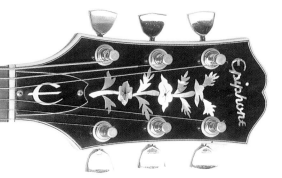

Pro set *(above) The unusual Professional amplifier could only be used when controlled by the Professional guitar. Effectively without any controls of its own, the amp* *had to be connected to the guitar with a special cable. This connection enabled the controls on the guitar to operate the amplifier's volume, tone, reverb and tremolo circuits.*

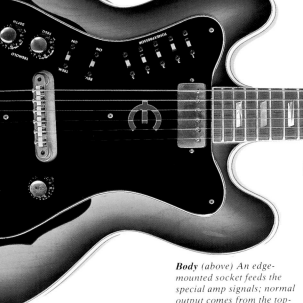

EPIPHONE PROFESSIONAL c1963

Serial: 126149
Professional produced 1962-1967

Pro *(above) Epiphone joined the early 1960s vogue for guitar gadgetry with this odd instrument. Fiddling with the line of five Tonexpressor switches gave rather haphazard tonal changes, while the special amplifier's settings could be adjusted from extra controls on the guitar.*

Body *(above) An edge-mounted socket feeds the special amp signals; normal output comes from the top-mounted socket.*

JON AND HOWARD

It's not often that I've had a chance to buy a guitar as unusual as the Howard Roberts from a shop in England, but some time on an early Yes tour, maybe 1973, in Manchester, Jon Anderson came to me and said, "I've seen a guitar down the road that I think you'll like, but I don't know what it is." I was notorious for the guitars, and it was spreading – Jon himself had started collecting, Chris Squire got into guitars as well as basses, and even drummer Alan White decided to start accumulating a few guitars.

So I went to see the guitar Jon had spotted... and it was this absolutely immaculate Howard Roberts – I think I paid around £400 for it. I would play it at home a lot, and I thought I was going to go further with it. At times I've wondered whether I should develop more of a relationship with it, so that I can pull it out of the bag, but so far it has no relevant recording history.

I had the Professional guitar and amp in my house in north-west London for ages, in what we called the music room. It was nice having a rare piece that you could play on. I bought it in England, probably in the late 1970s, in a music shop somewhere on the south-east coast, and I think I paid about £650 for the set. I really thought it was a serious solo performing guitar – you could actually play good Chet Atkins on it, the single pickup gave quite a jazzy tone. It looked great and sounded good. The switching system on the Pro is actually better than most 'gimmicky' set-ups: it works very efficiently, and having the reverb and tremolo controls on the guitar can occasionally be helpful.

ENCOURAGING CAIOLA

The funny thing about my Epiphones is that I've never really got totally into any of them. When I got the Caiola, with its switches and unusual sounds, I'd take it along to Yes rehearsals, pull it out and muck around with it, thinking that I'd eventually get something going with the guitar. The tone switches are a bit like those on the Fender Bass VI (p44) in that you can switch away and seemingly keep detracting from the sound you started with. It's an EQ system which really cuts into the sound of the guitar.

I thought the look of the Caiola worked, and if you like a guitar from the design point of view, then it already has something to live up to in the sound department. I liked the generally 335-style shape, and the neck felt really exciting, very encouraging. So I haven't given up on this one, it just hasn't been very useful in the practical sense. I find Epiphones less powerful electrically than Gibsons, but they do have a nice style and atmosphere about them, although they haven't really come through in my work.

I don't recall where I bought the Broadway, but the neck and fretboard were badly offset. So I had Sam Li work on the guitar for me, reshooting the fretboard and putting in block inlays. I saw it at the time as a sort of cheaper alternative to a vintage L5, because I liked the sound of an f-hole archtop guitar. But the Broadway never quite lived up to my expectations of it, and I tend to favour my L4C for that area of sound.

12-string *(right) At the same time as I got my blonde six-string (far right) from the Rickenbacker factory in the late 1970s, I also acquired this 12-string, featured here in a live shot. Unfortunately, it was one of a small batch of guitars that was stolen from my house a few years ago.*

4001 *(above) In contrast to the appeal of Rickenbacker's hollow-body guitars, most players prefer their solid-body basses, exemplified by the 4001. The model received a great boost in popularity during the 1970s when it was used so well by our bassist in Yes, Chris Squire.*

RICKENBACKER 1993 MODEL July 1964

Serial: DG869
1993 model produced 1964-1967

Rickenbacker *Swiss-born Adolph Rickenbacker set up his company in California in 1925. At first Rickenbacker made guitar parts, lap steels and amplifiers, and was among the first to market electric guitars. Modern-looking electrics appeared in the 1950s, and the brand really took off in the 1960s when groups like The Beatles and The Byrds used the distinctive sounds and looks of Rickenbacker. Many of the company's guitars have changed little, and much of their appeal today lies in their embodiment of the past.*

Body *(above) The proper f-hole, and not Rickenbacker's usual 'slash' hole, is only on 1960s UK export models.*

RICKENBACKER 4001 BASS October 1974

Serial: NJ6074
4001 produced 1961-current

*Neck (below) The
triangular position markers
are a distinctive feature of
many Rickenbacker
fingerboards.*

RICKENBACKER 360 August 1977

Serial: QH3291
'Modern' 360 produced 1964-current

*Six & 12 The 360 model
(above) has been a
mainstay of the
Rickenbacker line since
1958, first appearing in this
unbound-body format in
1964. The model is still
made in what Rickenbacker
calls its 'Old Style' bound-
body (like the 12-string in*

*the live pic, far left). The
Model 1993 (left) was an
export-only version of the
American 330-12 model. It
was part of a range made
specially for the UK market
in the 1960s, no doubt
prompted by The Beatles'
use of a number of
Rickenbacker guitars.*

RICKENBACKER 12-STRING

Quite recently I traded a prototype Martin solid electric in order to get the Rickenbacker export 12-string pictured on the left. I haven't really used it properly yet, largely because all my 12-string prayers were answered when the Steinberger arrived (see p62). But I'd enjoyed using my original 12-string (it's in the live shot at the top of the opposite page), and I was upset when it was stolen in 1987, along with three other guitars, a Prophet synth and a few other gizmos. I always keep an eye open for them, and I'd love them to turn up one day. The Rickenbacker 12 had serial 3672; the other three were a Fender Flame (serial unknown), an Ibanez guitar synth (K854495) and my Sixties sunburst Strat (165960).

When I got my original Rickenbacker 12-string, it was because I knew you couldn't get that sound from anything else. 'Awaken' on *Going For The One* was the first time that I ever tore into 12-string guitar, and the Rickenbacker 12 is a good deal of that track. It plays the strange-time riff – we never did things for too long in four-four

– and races through endless chord changes, because that part of the song, before the organ section, was an attempt by Yes to put in every basic chord. We would often use a musical vehicle to keep our music from the three-chord norm.

I had the original 12-string customised with holes in the back of the headstock so that you could thread strings through, and added a 12-piece bridge. I found its R-type tailpiece to be a complete disaster: I used to have to take off the tailpiece, thread all the strings in, stick them down with gaffer tape, put it back on, and then all the strings were loose and ready. There was no way you could thread-on a string while the tailpiece was still in position, so if you broke a string it was absolute hell.

FOUR AND SIX

I bought the 4001 bass new in England in 1975 for about £300 – I just suddenly decided that I had to have a Rickenbacker bass. I immediately did what a lot of people do with these, and took off

the pickup cover – otherwise you can't really get at it. And I've found that in the studio I need to merge together a bit of amp sound and a bit of direct injection to get the best from the 4001.

Most of *Beginnings* was recorded on that bass, and I used it on 'Never Say No' on *GTR* because the bass player, Phil Spalding, couldn't quite satisfy what everyone wanted, so I went and did it on the Rickenbacker. The 4001 bass also turns up on 'While Rome's Burning' and the title track on *Turbulence*, and 'Desire Comes First' on The *Grand Scheme Of Things*.

The blonde six-string I got direct from the Rickenbacker factory while we were on tour in California in 1977. I've not changed it at all, although sometimes it needs a bit of gaffer tape across the strings behind the bridge because they rattle – a profoundly Rickenbacker-type problem. I like to use this guitar for rhythm chords, as on 'Desire Comes First' on *Grand Scheme*, 'Circus Of Heaven' on *Tormato*, and 'One Step Closer' on *Asia*, exploiting the naturally aggressive sound of the guitar.

Steve Howe would like to thank:
Pete Alanoff; Pat Aldworth; Jim Archey; Mark Ashford; Pete Barnhart; Tony Bingham; Pete Brewis; Michael Carey; Scott Chinery; John Clarke; Mike Coles; Steve Dracup; PJ Deacy; Doug Ellis; Eugene Friess; Roger Giffin; Daryl Gilbert; Diane Gilmore; George Gruhn; Jim Halley; Hidenori Hayashi; Heritage Guitars; Pete Holmes; Pete Horner; Bob Johnson; Claude Johnson-Taylor; John Kelly; Sam Li; Llewelyn; Andy Male; John Marshall; Phil McDonald; George Mel; Bart Nagel; Claude Nobbs; Dalf Ostsetab; Tony Richardson; Steve Rouchier; Paul Sauerteig; Mike Saville; Ed Seelig; Michael Tait; Chris Wilde; Dave & Tom Wilkinson; Yossel; Jim Yukich.

Steve Howe dedicates this book to the memory of Joe Meek, Alan Murphy, Roy Pitt and Clive Skinner.

Tony Bacon would like to thank:
Julie Bowie; Lorena Alexander; Tony Bingham; Nigel Bradley; Walter Carter; Shelagh Cassidy; Paul Day; Roger Dean; Jim Deurloo; Peter Doggett; Gordon Duncan; Kevin Gray; Sue Hague; John Hall; Yoshika Horita; Alan Lewis; Mike Longworth; Lee-Ellen Newman; Emma Nickelwright; Debbie Orsland; Bill Puplett; Ian Purser; Maggie Simpson; Miki Slingsby; Steve Soest; Spanish Guitar Centre, London; Sally Stockwell; Nick Taylor; Will Taylor; Ray Ursell.

BIBLIOGRAPHY
TONY BACON (editor) *Rock Hardware* (Blandford 1981).
TONY BACON & PAUL DAY *The Fender Book* (Balafon/IMP 1992); *The Gibson Les Paul Book* (Balafon/IMP 1993); *The Ultimate Guitar Book* (Dorling Kindersley 1991); *The Guru's Guitar Guide* (Making Music 1990/92).
ROY BENNETT *GCSE Music Dictionary* (Longman 1990).
ANDRE DUCHOSSOIR *The Fender Stratocaster* (Mediapresse 1988); *The Fender Telecaster* (Hal Leonard 1991); *Gibson Electrics Volume 1* (Mediapresse 1981); *Guitar Identification* (Hal Leonard 1990).
TOM EVANS & MARY ANNE EVANS *Guitars: From the Renaissance to Rock* (OUP 1977).
MICHEL FOUSSARD (editor) *Guitares* (Collection Eurydice 1979).
PETE FRAME *The Complete Rock Family Trees* (Omnibus 1993).
GEORGE GRUHN & WALTER CARTER *Gruhn's Guide to Vintage Guitars* (GPI 1991).
FREDERIC V GRUNFELD *The Art and Times of the Guitar* (Da Capo 1969).
DAN HEDGES *Yes: The Authorised Biography* (Sidgwick & Jackson 1981)
COLIN LARKIN (editor) *The Guinness Encyclopedia of Popular Music* (Guinness 1992).
MIKE LONGWORTH *Martin Guitars, A History* (Four Maples Press 1988).
NORMAN MONGAN *The History of the Guitar in Jazz* (Oak 1983).
JOSE ROMANILLOS *Antonio de Torres* (Nadder 1987).
STANLEY SADIE (editor) *The New Grove Dictionary of Musical Instruments* (Macmillan 1984).
LARRY SANDBERG *The Acoustic Guitar Guide* (A Cappella 1991).
HARVEY TURNBULL *The Guitar From The Renaissance To The Present Day* (Batsford 1976).
TOM WHEELER *American Guitars* (HarperPerennial 1990).
RENE VANNES *Dictionnaire Universel des Luthiers* (Les Amis de la Musique, 1988).
THOMAS A VAN HOOSE *The Gibson Super 400* (GPI 1991).

PHOTOGRAPHS
All individual guitars were photographed by Miki Slingsby.

Other illustrations are listed below: page number/position/photographer/source (where applicable).
Position codes T=top, B=bottom, C=centre, L=left, R=right.

Jacket portrait: Miki Slingsby. 4-7: various. 8/BR/Miki Slingsby. 9/BL/Dave Richardson. 10/L/Miki Slingsby. 11/BL/Visuel 7/*The Gibson Story*. 11/BR/Miki Slingsby. 14/B/Miki Slingsby. 15/T/Tony Bacon/Gibson. 16/C/Visuel 7/*Beat Instrumental*. 16/B/Lisa Tanner. 17/T/Visuel 7/*Beat Instrumental*. 18/C/Visuel 7/*Guitar For The Practicing Musician*. 19/T/Miki Slingsby/*Guitar Player*. 20/L/Miki Slingsby. 21/T/Miki Slingsby. 21/B/Miki Slingsby/RCA. 22/B/Janet Howe. 29/TL/Visuel 7. 29/TR/Keith West. 29/B/Visuel 7/Rhino. 31/Miki Slingsby/Philips. 32/C/Miki Slingsby. 33/B/Paul Freehauf. 35/both/Miki Slingsby. 36/T/Dave Richardson. 36/B/Visuel 7/*Beat Instrumental*. 37/both/Miki Slingsby. 38/C/Neal Preston. 39/B/Visuel 7/*International Musician*. 40//B/Miki Slingsby. 41/TL(both)/Miki Slingsby. 41/CR/Bart Nagel. 42/C/Visuel 7/Fender. 45/T/Visuel 7/*Guitar Player*. 46/C/Tony Bacon/Capitol. 49/all/Miki Slingsby/BL:Ibanez. 50/both/Miki Slingsby. 52/T/Miki Slingsby. 56/B/Miki Slingsby. 57/T/Miki Slingsby. 58/both/Miki Slingsby. 59/B/Miki Slingsby. 60/C/Miki Slingsby. 66/C/Miki Slingsby/Columbia. 68/CL/Visuel 7/*Beat Instrumental*. 68/C/Martyn Dean. 68/BR/Tony Bacon/Jamie. 69/T/Martyn Dean. 70/BL/Visuel 7/Metronome. 70/CR/Tony Bacon/RCA. 71/TR/Miki Slingsby/RCA. 73/TR/Tony Bacon/*Melody Maker*. 73/B/Miki Slingsby. 76/T/Miki Slingsby/Martin. 76/BC/Paul Freehauf. 83/T/Miki Slingsby.